LOVED
CLOTHES LAST

LOVED CLOTHES LAST

How the Joy of Rewearing
and Repairing Your Clothes
Can Be a Revolutionary Act

ORSOLA DE CASTRO

PENGUIN LIFE

UK · USA · Canada · Ireland · Australia
India · New Zealand · South Africa

Penguin Life is part of the Penguin Random House group of companies
whose addresses can be found at global.penguinrandomhouse.com.

Penguin
Random House
UK

First published 2021
001

Copyright © Orsola de Castro, 2021

The moral right of the author has been asserted

Illustrated by Georgia de Castro Keeling, London, UK
Designed by Maria Maleh and Justin Moore, London, UK
Printed and bound in Great Britain by Clays Ltd, Elcograf S.p.A.

A CIP catalogue record for this book is available from the British Library

The authorized representative in the EEA is Penguin Random House Ireland,
Morrison Chambers, 32 Nassau Street, Dublin D02 YH68

ISBN: 978-0-241-46115-0

www.greenpenguin.co.uk

This book is for my husband Filippo, for my children Elisalex, Georgia, Giacomo and Leonia, for my grandchildren Vigo and Bronwen, and for my mother Matilde (Nanu).

LOVED
CLOTHES LAST

PREFACE

I started writing this book in October 2019. The week after I delivered the first draft to my editor, in February 2020, Milan went into lockdown as a result of the global pandemic of the coronavirus. To be even more precise, the day after I pressed Send I actually went to Milano Fashion Week, where I attended several shows and was a guest at a huge *Vogue Italia* gala dinner with hundreds of people.

Two weeks after I came back, London (where I live) went into lockdown too. By the time I was working on the final copy, in May 2020, I had been in self-isolation with my family, and most of the rest of the world, for more than two months.

In a few short months the world has been turned upside down, and many of the topics I talk about in this book – mass production and mass consumption, waste, the exploitation of workers and engaging thoroughly with modern technology – are now more relevant than ever.

INTRODUCTION

Fashion is not frivolous, it is actually incredibly important, and to define it just as a series of passing trends is to deny its fundamental role in human culture and history. Clothes have always been at the centre of our lives, marking our rituals, representing identity, profession, rank and status, but they have profound social implications as well. What we wear often brings us together with others who wear similar things, helping us to find our people, connect and belong. We have always been enamoured with our clothes, from the time when the primal instinct of covering up developed into a more sophisticated concept of adornment, and we show little sign of losing interest.

The modern-day fashion industry is huge: a maze of disconnected supply chains encompassing many other industries, from agriculture to communication, affecting 100 per cent of the population and touching lives, natural resources, people and places in equal measure. In the UK alone the industry is worth approximately £32 billion, providing more than 850,000 jobs. Globally we are looking at a US $2.4 trillion business of never-ending runs of tops, dresses, trousers, T-shirts, shoes, bags and bikinis – mostly looking the same, and many made by the same high-street or high-end enormous companies.

Fashion is one of the most socially exploitative and resource-polluting industries in the world, its economic and environmental impact is vast and its capacity for cultural influence is endless. Fashion is by no means superficial; it delves deep, saying as much about who we are, and the state of our civilization, as it does about our personal tastes and our local traditions.

Of course, its association with fleeting passions and women's work has rendered fashion an easy target for mockery, but the truth is that it cuts a much more serious figure in the great scheme of things, and today's fashion industry is hiding some pretty dark secrets behind a facade of gloss and glamour.

The statistics are almost grotesque: clothing production has doubled in the past 15 years and yet we are wearing our clothes less and less, either keeping them hidden and useless at the back of our wardrobe or getting rid of them without thinking of the consequences.

As a result, of the supposed 53 million tonnes of textiles produced globally every year, over 75 per cent are discarded, both in the production phase and at post-consumer level (after we've worn it). The equivalent of a rubbish truck full of discarded clothes goes straight into landfill every second.

The fate of cheap clothing is marked as soon as it leaves the factory, and it's worthy of an unedited Grimm Brothers fairy tale: made in misery, bought in haste, worn for one night (if that) and then chucked in the bin. Our ready-to-wear has turned into ready-to-waste. Karl Marx once said that religion is the opiate of the masses – to upgrade this concept, today's consumerism is our crack cocaine.

And expensive things aren't necessarily better made; the luxury sector is equally responsible for damaging the environment and for human exploitation, and it would be a big mistake to think that just because something costs more its profits are more ethically distributed throughout its supply chain.

There is not much difference, apart from the price tag, between cheap clothes and fast luxury. It is the entirety of the fashion industry that is called into question, as is our insatiable thirst for more, more, more.

MEND

'Over 75 per cent of the 53 million
tonnes of textiles

REPAIR

produced globally
every year are discarded.'

REWEAR

There is no way that we can continue like this, as our resources are finite and will soon be limited in availability – polyester will become more expensive than silk if we are to drastically reduce our dependency on fossil fuels, and cotton prices will skyrocket as we run out of the soil in which to grow it. Sustainability may be a buzzword right now, but what does it really mean to be sustainable when it comes to our clothes? What are the choices that we can all make, as clothes wearers, to shift from being part of the problem to becoming instead part of the solution?

It is wrong to think of sustainability as just another passing trend; the truth is very much the opposite: sustainability has been trending for billions of years, it is essential to our survival and our evolution. Sustainability is about balance, quality and respect; it denies us nothing and provides us with everything. It speaks of gratefulness rather than greed, resourcefulness instead of exploitation. Writer and activist Dominique Drakeford defines sustainability as 'an inherently black, brown and indigenous regenerative mechanism for living and engaging with nature'. Excess – that is the trend, and one we need to make firmly unfashionable or we are in danger of being the instruments of our own demise.

We can all do so much to change this. We can mend, repair and rewear. The alterations we must make aren't about enjoying things less, they are about enjoying things differently and, when it comes to our wardrobes, reclaiming and restyling our used clothes to shape our intentions. We can look at limitations not as restrictions but as ways to stimulate alternative solutions, challenging ourselves to think of imperfections and faults as opportunities for improvement, rather than something to be discarded; just as we can learn so much from a mistake, so a broken piece of clothing properly mended can become a favourite statement piece.

We don't have to go far to gather the knowledge to make our clothes last longer; a small generational rewind is enough, because reusing and recycling are as old as time, the knowhow is engraved in all cultures and we are hard-wired to it – only now the benefits and implications are wider than ever. We can employ used clothing as a metaphor for political expression (think the Sex Pistols, slogan T-shirts, badges, banners, patches, pussy hats and rainbows) and as a tool to reduce our carbon footprint, because rewearing and repairing encourage slower, more careful consumption patterns, fostering a culture of appreciation instead of exploitation.

The actions required are simple, not sweeping. And they give us infinitely more than they take away. The point is to start now, at your own pace, in your own way, and explore what it feels like to drape yourself in new ideas and old clothes.

This book is a call to action to use our clothes – and the tools that make them last – as our armour, taking up mending as a revolutionary act. At this important juncture we are between evolution and extinction, one road leading to ruin and one to redemption. We must do what is required of us as citizens, and that is to take action: small actions or big actions, all are welcome, all are necessary.

This is not a 'how to' book, it's more of a 'why to' – a book for making things and for making changes.

Chapter 1

Mending Is
a State of Mind

Clothes touch us all. We may not all be interested in fashion, but we can't avoid getting dressed, which means that every time we gaze into our wardrobes wondering what to wear, we could be making a choice that has a positive or a negative impact.

The global fashion industry is producing well over 100 billion garments per year (and that's not counting shoes, bags and other accessories), made from materials of unclear origins, by a workforce that is often inadequately paid, in disconnected, inefficient, opaque, often unsustainable and exploitative supply chains to feed our apparently insatiable 'consumer demand'.

Tonnes and tonnes of clothes reach stores and warehouses and leave stores and warehouses unsold (because there were too many), to go God knows where, to be incinerated or go into some other circuit of excess.

Judging by how many things are left unused and unloved, the less we know about the clothes we buy, the less we make an emotional connection and the easier it is to get rid of them – discarded items that we once desired, but did not cherish.

The fashion supply chain is not a land far, far away; we all become a part of it the moment we decide to buy something. Our responsibility is not limited to making sure that the stuff we buy is ethically and sustainably made, but also that it is ethically and sustainably disposed of – and that means keeping clothes for as long as possible and seeing our wardrobes as a starting point, not the finishing line.

Basically we cannot keep buying and throwing, hoping that at some point soon it will all disappear in a big closed-loop recycled rainbow. However, we can still consume – properly 'consume', from the Latin *consumere*, meaning 'to destroy or expend by use' – and, by implication, rewear, repair and commit.

'**I** The fact that mass production, mass consumption and accelerated disposal are scarring our planet and our culture is something that few people can doubt. And yet it is so hard to change, as we go about our daily lives weighed down with things: things we don't need, things we might not even really want, things that should be luxuries and not conveniences, because things that are permanent should be carefully considered.

And make no mistake: the items we buy and surround ourselves with really are permanent, in the sense that they were not designed to decompose or biodegrade, or turn into something else once their first function is over. Everything else in nature does, including us.

Antoine Delavoisier, considered to be the father of modern chemistry, said that in nature, nothing is created and nothing is destroyed, but everything is transformed. Our clothes pass through us and keep on living for a long time after we throw them away, because there is no 'away'. In fact, except for the small percentage of fibres that are turned back into other fibres (1 per cent, according to the Ellen MacArthur Foundation), everything you have ever owned, and thrown, is still here, in one shape or another: either enriching someone else's life, because it is true that one person's trash can be another person's treasure, or poisoning a landfill close to your home, or close to somebody else's home.

Maintenance is a word we no longer associate with clothing at all, but it lies at the crux of the problem, and is a way to define part of the solution, a way to redress the balance between consumption and disposal. For sure, repairing an object of value and fixing the hem of a £2.99 Boohoo miniskirt may feel oceans apart, but right now it's the attitude that counts. We shouldn't be measuring a garment's value by its price tag, but by the purpose it has in our life. We should own it because we love it, and because we love it we should want to keep it for ever, consume it, wear it to death.

To counteract disposable consumerism, the only way is to keep. Everything around

CHOOSE

us tells us to throw, so we should rise to the challenge and keep. Even if it costs me more to repair something than buying it new, I choose to keep.

HOW DID WE GET HERE?

The story of poorly made objects is well known: it started in the USA in the 1920s with General Motors, to encourage the buying of more cars, more often, and was originally intended as a way to increase production (and jobs) by deliberate manipulation of the design of a product, in order for it to break sooner.

This system is called 'planned obsolescence' (although the original name, as coined by the man who invented it, Alfred P. Sloan, Jr, was 'dynamic obsolescence'), and it has now spread to almost everything we buy – things are not made to last, and there are increasing legal or logistical loopholes that actively prevent us from independently repairing the stuff we buy once it breaks, as anyone in possession of a faulty iPhone or leaking washing machine knows only too well. You can't just call the person down the road to mend your broken object, because it wasn't designed to be disassembled: only approved technicians will do. Why?

The monopolizing, forceful and non-inclusive nature of this business model, which is directly responsible for our current cheap mass production and resulting crisis of hyper-consumerism, denies decent work to local communities. Repairing, crafts and making are no longer seen as dignified, viable professions, which in turn decreases our capability for manual skills, because we are no longer teaching such skills in schools.

The loss of skills and abilities that we have honed for millennia isn't just a sad cultural loss, it has also other implications, as does any loss to the overall ecosystem. Many of the manual skills required to be a surgeon – precision, a steady hand, needlework, accurate cutting, grafting – are not dissimilar to what is needed for domestic crafts – precision, a steady hand, needlework, cutting, folding. We are jeopardizing more than simply the demise of crochet

KEEP'

doilies and dodgy woodwork if we continue to nurture future generations that are manually capable of doing little more than scrolling down your feed.

'This

"ETHICAL FASHION"

this

"SUSTAINABLE FASHION"

that complies to
what fashion really is,
that is borne out of

PASSION, SKILLS, HERITAGE, ARTISTRY & BRAVERY

IS FASHION.

It's everything else that isn't.'

WHY MEND?

'Maintaining' and 'caring' are words that should be associated with everything we do, even if, in order to do so, we need to go out of our way, or outside our comfort zone. Some of the solutions are mere gestures – forgotten, everyday simple gestures – which is why it is so important to reclaim our time to relearn them.

Mending, for instance: it really isn't that difficult. Sure, there are any number of excuses as to why it's not convenient, but it's a small action that will take you on a big journey.

Take a broken zip. In my many years of scouring second-hand clothing sorting warehouses I have seen hundreds of perfect pieces abandoned simply because of a broken zip. After all, what is the point of spending time and money repairing a broken zip when ultimately it is cheaper, quicker and infinitely more fun to buy a new piece, with a fully functioning zip? But can we please stop and consider what we are actually doing when we give up hope on the one that broke? And what happens when we choose to mend it instead?

That broken zip, and the fabric that surrounds it, will either be confined to the back of your wardrobe (the average British woman hoards approximately £285 worth of unused clothing – the equivalent of £30 billion of useless purchases nationwide) or unceremoniously thrown away, despite the fact that 95 per cent of what we discard could be recycled or upcycled.

The piece you replace it with was probably made by a woman (80 per cent of garment workers are young females) in conditions that are, at best, exploitative (because none of the mainstream brands we see on our high street are paying their workforce a dignified living wage) and, at worst, downright life-threatening. The 2013 Rana Plaza factory collapse in Bangladesh killed 1,138 garment workers and injured more than 2,500, the deadliest industrial disaster in the fashion industry, but by no means the first, or the last.

If your garment was made from cotton, there is a very high risk that modern-day slavery was present in its production (more than £100 billion worth of garments at risk of being the product of forced labour were imported into G20 countries in 2017). If it contains polyester, each time you wash it, it will release hundreds of microfibres into the ocean (microfibres have been found everywhere, from the deepest ocean floor all the way to the top of Mount Everest).

On the other hand, if you decide to mend it, you will be challenging the system, because repairing something that was designed to be disposable is a statement against quantity vs quality. It will be challenging your lifestyle by introducing new habits that reduce your impact on the planet, because doubling the useful life of clothes from one to two years reduces their carbon footprint by 24 per cent.

It will take more time – you'll have to give it to someone else to do the job (I don't recommend changing zips at home, unless you are skilled), but that could be as close as your local dry cleaner. Yes, it will cost you probably only a fraction less than buying something new, but there is far more to mending a zip than the cost and effort, and many more systems are supported by the act of deciding to have zips mended, not thrown.

It is a person who mends your zip – a person with different skills from those you have, someone grateful for your custom; someone who, by virtue of a physical connection to the fabric of, say, your trousers, becomes connected to the fabric of your life; someone from your local community, someone tangible. It's a real transaction.

And what about the zip itself? Cheap, mass-produced zips attached to mass-produced clothes by poorly paid individuals working under pressure and overtime are not the same thing as a single zip, chosen to colour-match the one that broke and machine-sewn individually especially for you. That's a totally different zip experience, and it feels way better than the fleeting newness of a cheap pair of trousers in a plastic bag.

Lengthening the lifespan of clothes, and improving the things we own by caring for them when they break, means also striving towards an overall improvement of the system, and towards a fashion industry that considers the quality of the products we buy, and the quality of the lives of the people who make them.

Almost everything we buy right now is made in a hegemony of sameness, so customizing and personalizing things to be particular and different is a small but powerful act of sabotage – an antidote to wearing the same clothes as everyone else; your individualism shouting out to be seen.

ARE EXPENSIVE CLOTHES BETTER?

All this applies in exactly the same way when talking about luxury goods. It is a mistake to think that expensive clothes lead to fairly paid workers, or to significantly superior environmental standards: an expensive shirt may be made with luxurious fabrics, but it will likely be produced in the same factory clusters as the cheap one, by people who are unlikely to be better paid or working in dignified conditions; the materials used in its construction will be just as polluting, and its carbon footprint roughly the same. Sure, it will be better received at your local charity shop, but charity shops are brimming with our unwanted clothes anyway, because donating to charity is no longer an act of goodwill, but an act of dumping our responsibilities along with our unwanted clothes.

Whether you have 'invested' in a designer shirt or whether you buy high-street stuff, the same recipe applies: when it breaks, don't give it up – have it fixed. The shirt will benefit, your community will benefit, as will the planet and the people who make our clothes: because the act of caring for your clothes (as Joan Crawford said, 'Care for your clothes like the good friends they are') is a powerful signal for brands. Just as important as voting with your wallet, you are voting with your common sense, and you are saying: *Slow down, we have enough; we want better – not more.* See? You are starting to go somewhere way further than your local dry cleaner, because you are actively walking towards a more considerate, intelligent future.

There is so much more that you can explore, once you are a bit more confident that what you decide to do will make one hell of a difference. There are thousands of ways to mend broken clothes or to alter clothes that don't fit any more; and thousands of people and places – real or virtual – where you can learn how to do so.

'A FRESH GENERATION ARE MARCHING FOR REVOLUTION AND THEY WANT TO WEAR CLOTHES THAT TELL A NEW STORY.

LET'S GIVE IT TO THEM.'

Naomi Klein, social activist & author

Throughout history, clothes have been regularly thrashed, unpicked, resewn, rejuvenated, reconditioned, cut up, repurposed, revived, reworn and remade, because, until quite recently, frugality and efficiency made economic sense: clothes were expensive, designed to last, and their wearers were implicit in their longevity, repurposing and upcycling not as a fashion statement, but as a result of poverty, ingenuity and need. Unfortunately, rather than celebrating the creativity and the craft of maintaining, we have always focused on the shame of poverty and need; wearing hand-me-downs and make-do-and-mend suffer from a worldwide, age-old cultural blanket of negative associations spreading from Mexico to China: poor people wear old stuff, rich people buy new.

How absurd that it is now precisely the opposite, with vintage and pre-loved clothes, mending and customizing as the niche, elitist, conscious option, and buying masses of cheap new stuff as the affordable, democratic solution. It is vital that we defy and redefine the negative stigma around (further) consuming used clothes from the unacceptable to the aspirational; and if our parents, grandparents and great-grandparents perceived second-hand as a badge of shame, we now need to turn it into a badge of pride: we aren't repurposing and mending clothes because we can't afford to buy something new – we are doing it because we can't afford to throw something away. What has made economic sense for previous generations will make environmental sense for generations to come.

Clothes are our chosen skin. We can use them to speak of our principles, demand positive change and make sure that what makes us feel good about ourselves is also an instrument to bring good to others. Alexander McQueen spoke about fashion as a reflection of the world we live in, and any old photograph will prove it – we can instantly date an image from its subjects' outfits. For those of you who were alive in the 1980s, for instance, the layering of several cut-up T-shirts that looked so cool on Madonna or, before that, punks (ripped tartan, studs and safety pins) and hippies (crochet squares and embroidered jeans), the New Romantics (vintage Victorian petticoats dyed black with everything) and the whole Grunge thing (more crochet squares and embroidered jeans) – these are all testaments to youth taking up scissors and needles to customize, in order to rebel, and saying something by looking different.

I CARE,

I REPAIR

Today, at the dawn of Generation Climate Breakdown, the 'I Care, I Repair' and #lovedclotheslast message that we share when we mend and alter our clothes has gone beyond showing off sartorial originality and *savoir faire*; it is now a statement that the act of caring for our clothes extends to the act of caring for our environment, and marks our gratitude by valuing the work of the people who make the things we wear.

If we look at this shift as a mass endeavour to embrace a more 'conscious' consumerism, we need first to understand that being conscious opposes being unresponsive and implies action over apathy.

Positive action can take several forms, and becoming a clothes-keeper is by far one of the easiest and most rewarding.

FIRST-AID BASICS
FOR CLOTHES

HEMS
☞ It is pretty easy to pick up a dropped hemline: you can find numerous tutorials online. Provided the thread you use matches the fabric, nobody will really notice even the most cack-handed attempt (unless it's an evening piece or something special, and then you might want to have it done professionally).

☞ But don't confuse a hem and the internal overlock, which is needed to prevent fabrics from fraying. Overlocking is harder to contain once it starts unravelling, as it's sewn with three or four different threads. Cheap overlocking is often not secured, so I always suggest turning a garment inside out before buying it: if there are tiny threads or loose threads, pull them. If they start to unravel, don't buy it. ✂

BUTTONS
☞ Personally, I find sewing buttons extremely relaxing, but in case you don't, that problem can be solved by your local dry cleaner.

☞ New buttons can transform a cheap shirt into one that is completely unique to you, by making the buttons the feature.

☞ A quick browse on Google and you'll find loads of buttons in different shapes and colours, and unless you decide to splash out on vintage ones, you can get them very cheaply. Car-boot sales are also great button-hunting territory. ✂

EMBRACING THE FRAY

There is hope even for the laziest among us, because ultimately you could do nothing at all and let your clothes fade without intervention. For me, wear-and-tear is symbolic of a personal, individual path, with breakages (mended or raw) as a powerful visualization of our activities, memories of moments, the scars of our everyday, an integral part of our clothes' stories.

Aesthetically, there is a lot going for the 'worn-out' look. Except that we aren't wearing our clothes long enough to wear them out; instead we prefer to buy things that are mass-produced to *look* used – another strange modern-day dichotomy, whereby time is so scarce (or we think it is) that we are losing the habit of owning clothes that will accompany us and deteriorate as a consequence of the life we live.

Why is it okay to pay someone next to nothing to work in precarious and unsafe surroundings to make it look as if you did unspeakable things to your jeans, but not okay to impose your own natural wear-and-tear on other wardrobe staples? Factory-made, chemically distressed denim is one of fashion's utmost stupidities, and we will look at its implications a little later on, but it doesn't really make sense that jeans should be allowed to look great while falling apart, while shirts, T-shirts, knits and dresses aren't allowed to age in the same way.

I possess several pieces (and I use the word 'possess' rather than 'own' to emphasize how much I love these clothes) that I leave untouched in their very visible deterioration because, in my opinion, they look more elegant as they fade. In particular, my ripped black silk 1940s tea-dress, a green cashmere cardigan that belonged to my paternal grandmother, which is literally becoming a hole, and a pair of vintage black wool trousers fraying and splitting at the hems: pieces that are aesthetically benefiting from use and on which I maintain a deliberate no-repair policy.

Of course, it helps that these items are beautifully made from exquisite materials, because you can see quality in the way the garment is sewn and how the fabric thins; each hole, each tear and each thread that emerges as time goes by displays unfolding stories (it started fraying in Rome; that nightclub rip in Brixton; the Thailand tear).

I often wear them for evenings, with heels and jewellery (as polished as possible), emphasizing the imperfection as the defining detail:

- ☞ **A pair of trousers** that are fraying at the hems, and one leg is split almost to the knee. I will add sheer black or patterned tights and killer shoes.
- ☞ **A jumper** that is covered in holes and so broken up at the elbows that one arm is almost hanging by a thread. I will work on what's underneath it.
- ☞ **A dress** that is so faded it's gone from black to dark grey and is totally torn. I wear it with a string of pearls and red nail varnish.

I belong to the lazy category when it comes to all this mending malarkey: I am good at sewing buttons, half decent at first-aid repair and very good at crochet, but that's it. Furthermore, years in the clothes-making business have cemented my conviction that I will never, ever learn how to sew convincingly! Nevertheless, looking after my clothes is easy and satisfying; a reminder that I don't have to go far to think outside the box – a completely doable everyday act of preservation that saves my wardrobe, and my soul.

Whether you have it mended or learn how to mend it yourself, or you let it go into its own broken oblivion, your clothes are your clothes and they should stay your clothes for a long time; and that's a big mindset change from where we are now, and one that will require some struggle. I hope this book will help you pick your battles.

Chapter 2

Rewind, Relearn, Resist

Making changes always requires some kind of bravery, and altering our habits is often an unsettling thing to do. Right now we are facing one of the greatest threats to our evolution – climate heating – so adapting our behaviours to a novel set of requirements will have to become a new habit very soon, as we shift towards a less polluting society.

With this book, I hope to inspire you to form brand-new habits (like using modern technology, apps and platforms to develop better buying mechanisms) and recycle a few old ones (like maintaining and preserving the things you bought, and slowing down your consumption). This isn't about ditching all that is fun and exciting in buying clothes, and it's not about deprivation; but it is about balance, thinking and acting. It's about discovering the joy and satisfaction of mending things yourself, the sense of purpose that comes from appreciating the things you own, and the free-spiritedness that accompanies positive action.

Above all, it is about drastically rethinking what is convenient, and perhaps discovering that the efforts required to make changes aren't quite as cumbersome as we have been led to believe. It will take some commitment, and some practical and creative thinking, but what needs to be done are simply a set of achievable actions that can easily be integrated into our daily lives.

REWIND

I don't think it's too implausible to say that as soon as human beings learned how to weave, we also learned how to darn, and that very shortly after we mastered the craft of making, we set out discovering how to mend. In fact when we look at textiles and clothes, the need to conserve them has been a catalyst of continuous innovation – from something as basic as turning a coat inside out to wear it twice as long, to the invention of chemically derived, durable materials such as nylon and polyester.

In the craft of reuse we encounter the jaw-dropping, awe-inspiring connection between arts and crafts, that point where an object takes on (another) life of its own, the moment when object and owner fall into symbiosis, via the damage, through the repair.

Why did we go so spectacularly wrong that this basic instinct now needs to be relearned? Why did we succumb to a culture that tells us that buying lots of new stuff is directly linked to happiness and fulfilment? Stockpiling lots of clothes leads to wardrobe clutter, not personal gratification, and considering that the majority of the clothes that are bought today are cheap to buy and cheaply made, serialized and identical, they don't inspire the respect and love that are a fundamental part of emotional ownership, together with the desire to make things last, care for them and repair them when they break.

And yet when we talk about clothes, we are talking about the skin we choose to wear, both our protection *from* the outside world and our projection *to* the outside world. I don't think covering up was the result of some shame at being naked, but I do think it quickly became linked with pride about our appearance. To the same degree by which we are what we eat, we also are what we wear.

To understand our deep relationship with fabric we need to look no further than our languages, and how often we use textile-inspired terms as metaphors to describe everyday occurrences, which is why in this book I want to talk about threads:

'We weave conversations and unravel complexities;
we knit together thoughts, as well as jumpers.'

visible threads, invisible threads; threads for making and threads for mending; threads that structure clothes and threads that structure thoughts; threads that connect, and broken threads that need to be reconnected. Because threads are so much more than just fabric filaments.

Think about relationships that come with 'no strings attached'; 'living on a shoestring'; the patchwork of our communities; and the fabric of our society. We weave conversations and unravel complexities; we knit together thoughts, as well as jumpers.

We are told to consider that 'clothes don't make the person' and are counselled 'not to air our dirty laundry in public', and this rich tapestry of oral wisdom is repeated all over the world, with local versions of similar sayings. In France and Italy they metaphorically use the age-old habit of wearing your jacket inside out to make it last longer – *'retourner sa veste'* and *'volta gabbana'* – to describe someone who has changed their mind; and in Spain something simple to do is as easy as *'cortar y coser'* (cutting and sewing). In Zimbabwe being 'about to take one's clothes off' is to say that the end is near; in Aruba they lament that 'not all clothes are dried in the sun'; and in Kazakhstan you congratulate someone by bidding them to 'wear it a long time'.

For me personally, the conviction that 'it's not the pearls that make the necklace, it's the string' has been a guiding light since I was small, reminding me that substance and continuity are more important than sparkle and shine.

Reusing and repurposing were so endemic up until quite recently that they were designed into our lives. From cookery to crockery, from mosaic to patchwork, reclaiming leftovers and repairing the broken was an everyday occurrence: keeping was the default, and throwing was a failure.

Today we are inundated with a constant stream of new things available to buy, and we have forgotten the value of having something old to save. When it comes to mending, we should cradle this concept like a sick child and bring it back to life, because we resolutely don't mend any more – we have forgotten how to in just a few short generations. The loss of this skill is devastating: it's like giving up. By contrast, reclaiming it is an elixir for immortality, a powerful visualization of our willingness to make a contribution to slowing down the fashion system. Mending speaks: How did you break that? A garment mended multiple times reads like a photo album, with the moments and memories that we stitch upon our clothes.

We have forgotten how to mend because it hasn't felt important. It is.

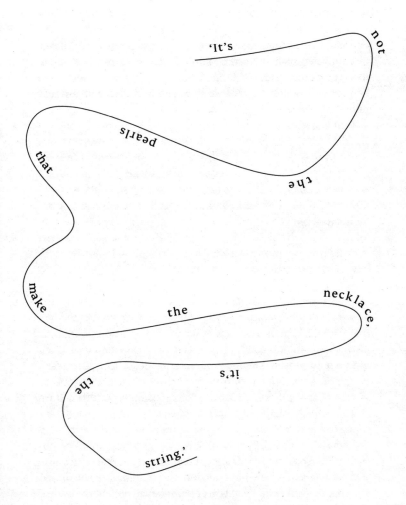

'It's not the pearls that make the necklace, it's the string.'

AESTHETICS/ETHICS

Our culinary cultures are steeped in reuse, and numerous dishes rely on yesterday's leftovers (think paella in Spain, minestrone in Italy, bubble & squeak in the UK), and many of the aesthetics and cultural references that we surround ourselves with are part of the same concept.

Think back to the last time you visited a trendy eatery – references to reclaiming are everywhere, in food chains and expensive restaurants alike, from tables made with recovered planks to mismatched crockery, or cocktails served in jam jars.

When it comes to modern art, the endemic reuse of found and discarded objects as an inspiration and as a technique is commonplace, reinvented for every generation by artists such as Michelangelo Pistoletto and, more recently, Olafur Eliasson. This is evident in the music industry too, with artists sampling other musicians' previous work within their own.

At today's fast pace, and in this present culture that values the new more than the old, the rough and patched might be only a look and no longer an everyday philosophy of life, but the fact that we still surround ourselves with it is important, because it proves that we find comfort in it, and we understand it; and it's everywhere – from 'shabby chic' interior decor to ripped jeans (much more on that later), from our homes to the high street.

One of the earliest and most brilliant examples of this culture is *wabi-sabi*, a philosophy that originated in Japan in the 14th century: the term *wabi-sabi* roughly translates as 'poverty' and 'loneliness', and visually it is all about the glorification of the objects of the poor, but the concept that it fostered is one of richness and abundance, where imperfection and fragility are celebrated for what they are: manifestations of difference, not inferiority.

From *wabi-sabi* came *kintsugi*, the craft of mending broken crockery with a gold amalgam to emphasize and romanticize the breakage; and *boro* fabric, intricate patchworks made from kimono leftovers (kimonos were dyed with indigo, which was expensive, therefore scraps were considered far too precious to dispose of, despite generational wear-and-tear); both techniques speak about the act of repairing as almost sacred, and both celebrate the triumph of life after death, of reconstruction after destruction.

Nowadays, original *boro* fabric is highly covetable, and a quick google will show you why – it looks just like the distressed and mended denim that is so fashionable today. You could use it as inspiration for customizing that pair of jeans in the back of your wardrobe, which you bought but aren't wearing, or to repair the ones that you wore too much. Keep patching, *boro* says, keep using; it challenges, because the story of your life happening on your trousers is something that you will want to remember.

HOW TO MEND YOUR JEANS

BORO-STYLE

☞ *Boro* is all about layered fabric scraps used as patches, reinforced with rows of running stitch, to mend, salvage and give new strength to old clothes that are damaged.

☞ If you have a tear in your jeans, start by pinning a scrap of fabric at the front and back of the tear. The fabric scraps need to fully cover the tear and extend beyond it all round, so that the patches can be secured to the denim around the tear.

☞ Take an embroidery needle and some white embroidery floss and, from the right side, hand-sew row upon row of running stitch across the entire patch, securing it to the denim and the backing patch. ✌

Of course, this kind of repair wasn't happening exclusively in Japan. The history of patchwork dates as far back as 5,000 years ago, having been discovered in tombs in China and Egypt. In the West quilting was alive and kicking, and travelling from Scotland to Virginia with the first pioneers.

Quilting, like *boro*, has inspired much more than simply design, and its influence can be seen from high fashion to contemporary art. Quilting acts as a stronger symbol than its folk-art aesthetics might suggest; it is a metaphor of close connections and even closer collaboration, as women across the generations would work together to create something precious, sharing secrets, experiences, joys and traumas in the process of making an heirloom.

The good news is that patchwork quilting is still very much alive, with no shortage of places where one can learn the basics; groups that you can join to experience at first hand what it must have felt like to sit and stitch together; and a hugely active online quilting community. Armed with a stack of treasured fabric scraps (think baby clothes, your grandad's shirts or even old cushion covers and worn fabrics that are too pretty to chuck out) and even the most rudimentary of sewing skills, you can start a memory quilt. At its core, quilting is a timeless, traditional and nostalgic pastime; one about slowing down, preserving fabrics and the memories stored within, but one that can be infinitely interpreted according to your individual vision and aesthetic.

Patchwork designs can be as simple as multiple squares, or as intricate as combining triangles, hexagons and rhombuses. You will also need wadding, or batting, and, in short, it can get complicated. I certainly don't know how to do it, although I adore quilts, so this is on my bucket list for sure. What I can do is tell you that all those sheets and pillow covers that tore or that you aren't using, an old forgotten *boho* skirt, men's shirts and flowery dresses can all be cut up and saved to nestle into a future quilt. Otherwise, you can get inspired by experts such as Kaffe Fassett and Anna Maria Horner, or fall down one of the many #quilting rabbit holes on Instagram or Pinterest.

'Our entente with nature will be re-written and re-invented; we will try to live together in a more harmonious way, giving and taking and caring for one another. A more intimate and intuitive relationship will be the result, based on primitive emotions, ancient rituals and archaic systems, re-inventing animism.' Li Edelkoort, trend forecaster, Bloom, issue #24: 'Earth Matters'

Quilting, *boro*, *kintsugi* and all these wonderful techniques that were devised so that we could keep things longer, so that our scraps and leftovers could attain glory – and so that our memories, as well as our valued resources, could stay with us for longer – are having a revival.

Despite Li Edelkoort's most recent predictions, we are nowhere near this level of appreciation of our present objects to imagine such a predominant, widespread impulse to keep, but what is interesting is how the aesthetic behind this philosophy – the 'look' that surrounds the principle – is still completely relevant in today's culture.

Right now, this look is definitely having its moment; catwalks are awash with the 'upcycled' look, and its vibrant, patchy, colourful, often idiosyncratic juxtapositions look great online: a breath of fresh air to contrast black and beige minimalism. Sure, for some designers it doesn't go further than a visual reference that suits their momentary design ethos, but for others it is a way to utilize their creativity to speak about things that are meaningful to them, such as slowing down the system or antagonizing mass consumerism.

To most consumers, this aesthetic language isn't speaking clearly yet – not as powerfully as a Katharine Hamnett T-shirt with 'SAVE THE FUTURE' emblazoned on it – but in the actual future (that is, if we do manage to save it), understanding that a piece of clothing made from several other pieces is a way to prevent more clothing being unsustainably disposed of can enhance the clothes we wear to become our personal manifesto. At a time when billions of items of clothing are delivered from factories annually, and while we embark on a journey of collective actions to search for solutions, the policy to care, to rewear and to repair is a real alternative.

MENDING IS A REVOLUTIONARY ACT

Mending techniques themselves have an intrinsic beauty, requiring precision combined with resourcefulness, and this aspect is what appeals to me, because if we look at mending through that lens, we can clearly see that each piece we repair is spectacular, unique, the product of artistry, invention and our time.

Making mending visible is a declaration of intent. It's like taking repairing your clothes to the same level as tattooing your skin. The current system we all know is telling us that if an item is broken, we should throw it away – only this time you say: *No, I want to keep it; in fact I want to keep it and mend it, and use it again and again*. If we are what we wear, then we should show what we mean; and we mean to mend our trousers as we mend our environment; we will repair our broken clothes and the broken systems alike.

I DON'T EVER SEE THE POINT TO

INVISIBLE MENDING

Celia Pym, textile artist

MENDING TECHNIQUES

Darning

If you look at mending as a purely practical endeavour, then darning is just lots of little lines of thread connected and woven in order to strengthen a spot that has become thin or damaged with wear. But if you take it as a vehicle to imagine other meanings, darning tells so many stories; and when it comes to the message we want to convey about the way we choose to interact with our clothes, it conveys our principles as well as any slogan T-shirt: *I care, I repair*.

Darned jumpers are completely in tune with today's looks: textures juxtaposing, colours clashing, a little rough around the edges. It is a technique that has accompanied us for millennia, its usefulness never questioned, until now. Newness is overrated; darning is experience, life and the passing of time. I love how it can be both modern and ancient all at the same time.

To me, darning speaks a thousand words, just because it looks so much like a mini-universe all of its own. There are several different mending techniques that are better suited to different materials, because darning, in my opinion, really does work best on knitted or loosely woven materials.

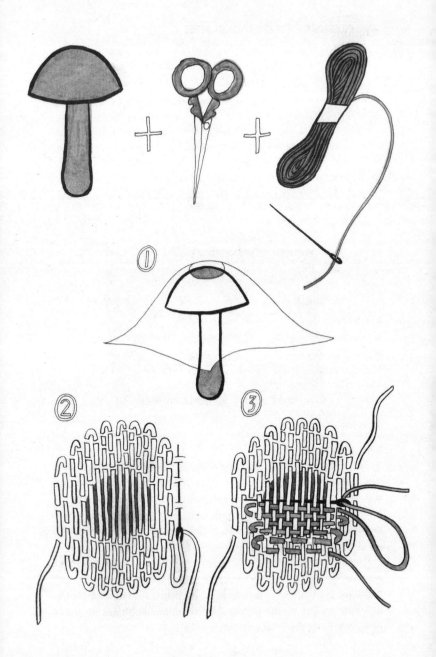

Patching

You've seen *boro*-style patches above, but you can patch any hole with almost anything, provided you follow the original fabric. For example, patch jersey and stretchy fabrics with an equally stretchy fabric, and it's best to use woven fabrics to patch other woven items. I quite like very roughly stitched patches, just like a child would draw, with long, sparse and irregular stitching to hold a (preferably) slightly frayed and uneven patch – but you can make them look super-neat if you hem or blanket-stitch the patch first, then sew it on less visibly. Or you could go online and look for ready-made patches, which you can then apply yourself.

Embellishing

This is the craft of adding something to improve on a piece that has seen better days, or to cover up a blemish or defect by adding to it, rather than fixing or covering it up. You can sew on beads, buttons, trims and any other dinky bits you might have lying around, or you can use embroidery.

My favourite jumper of all time is a black cashmere cardigan (my maternal grandmother's from the 1940s), which has been rescued with all of the above: black jersey elbow-patches, careful embellishing with tiny black beads, crocheting around moth holes, little embroidery motifs to complement some older darning, and a lace trim along the front to reinforce the hold of the buttons.

Heartbreakingly, nowadays, mending is almost obsolete. I was reminded of this at a recent event that I curated in Copenhagen, at which we placed a massive repair station, complete with mountains of fashion waste, machine operators and expert menders, bang in the middle of a high-fashion trade fair. As part of the three-day programme we held several 'open to the public' workshops on everything from repairing denim to embroidery, and I was surprised to see how many young people attended and practised. I took a photograph that is, by today's standards, almost absurd, of two young guys who had never taken up a needle and thread in their lives learning how to embroider and becoming completely engrossed in their new-found skill. It strikes me that it would have been less surprising to have seen a dodo walking past than two 16-year-old boys mending their trousers.

Because mending has become a rarity and an exception, we need help to bring it back, just like when animals at risk of extinction are supported to keep reproducing to save their species; we need designers to rethink their products to make them more mending-friendly, we need educators to take on the task of revaluing the craft of making and mending, and we need policies mandating that brands take responsibility for the clothing – and the waste – they produce. But most of all we need to upscale and diversify mending so that it becomes widely available for all, not simply hidden in full view in the windows of a few local dry cleaners, but visible and in its full glory as the brilliant thing it truly is. Think cool mending stores on every high street, and repair stations in supermarkets and department stores.

RELEARN

THE STIGMA

Breaking the stigma around mending is an important mental exercise, as it will change our assumptions about people with non-disposable income.

For generation upon generation, wearing hand-me-downs and visibly repaired clothing was a profoundly humiliating reminder of an inferior situation – of not being good enough to be clad in new clothing, due to restricted personal circumstances. And that was because for generation upon generation, cheap clothing bought in stores looked dreadful, and not everyone had mothers or aunts who were willing and able to machine-sew to make clothes from Burda and other cheaply available paper patterns.

Now we berate fast fashion as the symbol of evil, with activists across the globe demanding anything from bans to boycotts. I wish we were more careful in our thinking and recognized that we do need fashionable clothes that are affordable to be bought by the majority of the world's population. We need them to clothe our families, as we need them to support the families of the people who make them. We need a system where fast fashion, precisely because it has grown out of all control, can rebalance itself in order to thrive; we want cheap clothing that is made with dignity, and which doesn't cost the earth. We need a system where profits, and quality of life, are more equally distributed throughout the supply chain, as opposed to making a very few people very rich.

It takes a garment worker on a minimum wage in Bangladesh about **2 MONTHS** to earn what the highest-paid fashion CEO earns in **1 MINUTE**.

That is why we must be careful not to be too prescriptive in our call to arms and must manage our expectations: learning how to mend and repair is not for all, and making it *heroic* could smack of exclusivity, because in a throwaway society and at today's speeded-up pace, there risks being equal shame levied on those who cannot afford to buy anything other than cheap clothing and who can't afford the time it takes to repair something broken.

Now that the enemy is disposability and newness, and not longevity, wearing cheap clothing risks becoming the stigma of tomorrow: an immediate identification of poverty, just as repaired or reused clothing was, barely half a century ago. Fashion repeats itself in a constant cycle of reinvention, looking back into its trends and re-offering them every 20 years or so to a new, nostalgic generation. But not these trends, please. Let's make exclusivity, excess and lack of diversity the trends we will never, ever revive.

There is also a misconception that cheap fashion is so badly made that it doesn't warrant saving; that there is no point in investing time and money to repair something that costs so little and is made so poorly. I question this. As someone who buys for love and not on impulse, it is irrelevant to me the amount of money that I spend, when it comes to my emotional relationship with the piece I bought: everything I buy is worth keeping. I mend my Primark dress as I do my vintage Pucci. I wash my Victoria's Secret bra the same as my La Perla: by hand, with care and attention to detail.

BFF (BEFORE FAST FASHION)

Before fast fashion, cheap clothing was poorer in fabric and style, but often quite beautifully made. My favourite store, ever, in my whole life, was MAS (Magazzino allo Statuto) in Rome, a three-floor department store selling vast quantities of cheap, original pieces from their own stock, starting from the late 1960s, together with more up-to-the-minute pieces, for men, women and kids.

In essence, as well as buying in new pieces from current seasons, MAS also continued to sell all previously unsold stock, repurposing it on rotation from their own warehouses in a continuous cycle. And inside those clothes, in their labels, fashion history unfolded.

Up until the 1990s, and rigorously throughout the 1970s and '80s, the vast majority of the clothes were made in Italy, of impeccable quality and a somewhat goofy style, which of course I loved precisely because it was a bit oddball, like those retro ads in the endpages of Sunday supplements, with models sporting ridiculous hairstyles and tacky outfits.

I own at least five pairs of menswear trousers from MAS and, sure, the fabrics aren't luxury, they're either recycled wool or a wool-and-nylon mix, but the cut and the make would shame many 'premium' and 'luxury' brands of today, with exquisite attention to detail, in-built customization in the seams so that they could be adapted in time, big hemline allowances to allow for length alteration, pockets inside pockets – a make that was almost on par with real tailoring.

The same applied to women's clothes; even if inevitably made in 100 per cent nylon or other acrylic fabrics (although they did have the best 100 per cent cotton underwear and the most amazing 100 per cent wool vests), skirts, shirts and dresses were constructed to perfection and were always the perfect fit. Lacking in style maybe, but respectful to quality and time, because despite the fact that the clothes were made to be inexpensive, they were still made to last.

And then, come the 1990s, in came the invasion of cheap, copycat, stylish, on-trend fashion imported first from China and then from Bangladesh, and out went the cheap, tacky 'made in Italy' clothes – we know the rest. MAS, like many other department stores worldwide, closed in 2018.

SO HOW DID WE GET INTO THIS MESS?

In 1972 US President Nixon arrived in China and met Mao Tze-tung, forever altering global power structures and opening up China to the rest of the world after centuries of seclusion. Slowly what had been barriers became trade opportunities, and global industries began to move to new, undiscovered and largely unregulated shores. At that point, fashion brands still largely owned their producing factories, or worked in close proximity to their mills and manufacturers, creating a sense of community as well as protecting their intellectual property and USPs. In fact, in several cases the factories that were responsible for producing some of the best-known names in fashion ended up launching their own propositions: Alberta Ferretti and Ermenegildo Zegna are such examples.

However, as sewing skills and capabilities in Chinese-operated factories grew, it didn't take long for the fashion industry to cotton on to the huge potential that an exploited, non-unionized workforce and zero environmental protection would have on margins and profits. Over the course of the late 1980s and throughout the '90s, most of the technical knowhow, as well as the machinery accumulated in over 200 years of industrialization, moved to China. In some cases overnight.

This I did see happen, in person: in the late 1990s I was collecting most of the fabrics for my upcycled collections from Italian factories' surplus and excess, particularly around the Veneto region, which was then globally renowned as one of the iconic hubs of the 'made in Italy' label.

One particular mill – a beautiful, family-run business that had helped drive local employment and prosperity for a century, but had been struggling with increased competition – was forced to close, and all production was moved to China. The factory workers left for their Christmas holidays and when they eventually went back to work in January, the factory had closed and all the machinery was gone, transported to China, together with all manufacturing operations.

And yet, at that point, things could have moved in a very different way. Imagine if designer brands had discovered that a cheap overseas workforce and a lack of environmental laws and regulations presented a business, as well as a humanitarian, opportunity to create dignified jobs, improve the lives of millions of new workers and create designer diffusion lines that were considerably cheaper, but still with an emphasis on quality and design: would we have fallen for fast fashion if that had been the case, or would it have led to a more balanced equation between expensive and affordable?

'Fast fashion' has been accused, since its inception, of copying designer pieces (intellectual property in fashion being remarkably difficult to protect) and of placing those products right under our very noses. Unsurprisingly, we couldn't get enough, and that was the intention. Would we have wanted cheaply made designer copies at ridiculously low prices if we could have had the real deal – that is, actual designer clothes, but at more affordable price points?

Mass production was intended to generate, not feed, conspicuous consumption. We aren't hard-wired to buy, or hoard clothes; we have been herded, like sheep, to our closest high-street stores.

Things haven't become valueless, but we have come to see them as such. Sure, they are cheaper, less well made, but it is the way we interpret them that determines their worth. Because the truth is that we do need cheap, stylish, fashionable clothing for those who can't afford to spend money on fashion; we do need a democratic system whereby the entire clothes-wearing population has access to decently priced clothing that doesn't humiliate the people who make them and degrade the environment. It is the brands' responsibility to ensure that cheap clothing is made by workers who are unionized and paid decently, and is made with materials that have a regenerative effect on our environment, rather than depleting our resources (as materials can account for up to 95 per cent of a garment's environmental impact).

Finally, it is our responsibility to take care of the things we own, once we own them, and therefore to make sound decisions at every step of our ownership journey, from the first inkling of desiring a garment, to what we need to look out for at the purchasing point, to responsible disposal.

I always say that fast fashion is like a one-night stand: a non-committal dipping in and out without developing feelings; and that when it comes to our clothes, we need to start looking for committed relationships: bonds that will last for a lifetime of wear (and tear).

You want a piece that suits your figure to fit your principles, too. If it fits your shape as well as your values, then buy it. If not, press Pause and think again.

RESIST

NEEDLEWORK IS WOMEN'S WORK

The fact that sewing, mending and the domestic crafts in general were so closely associated with women's work may also be a reason for their inevitable decline, as they tied women firmly to a world of drudgery and domestic enslavement. As we looked towards emancipation from the stereotypes that impeded our freedom, it isn't surprising that, together with burning bras, many women relinquished the desire to be as we were.

The time has come to revalue old wisdoms and techniques and inject them with a fresh perspective, by turning oppression into opportunity. In a patriarchal system and gender-discriminating society, which has consistently shut down women's voices across the globe and throughout history, sewing became women's silent language, and I say that we can reclaim our legacy and use needlework to make our point.

Female artists have long been inspired by the idiosyncratic relationship with threads and fabrics, and by the role that women have had in being tied to them, and defined by them at the same time, as exemplified in the work of female artists such as Maria Lai, Dayanita Singh and Louise Bourgeois. It is as if the repetitiveness of sewing is a chore, but also a form of deep spiritual enlightenment. More recent phenomena, such as Craftivism (more on this in Chapter 3), are playing a vital role in redefining and repurposing this silent language and turning it into the loudest voice possible.

To do this, we need to tell ourselves a different story, one that speaks of empowerment and solidarity, and of getting together in mutual support for a common cause. We need to change the stigma: that flowery sewing kit with pincushions, dinky scissors, thimbles, needles and threads? Reimagine it, redesign it, bring it up to speed, both practically and metaphorically.

NOT CRAFTY

We must also be respectful of those of us who aren't mending-inclined, because plenty of us aren't by nature, or can't because of time, career or physical constrictions; and we must encourage a system where repair and mending are once again institutional-ized, part of the geo-fabric of our streets and communities. Here are a few ideas to mull over:

☞ Use your local dry cleaner as a starting point.
☞ Send your broken item back to the brand that made it (badly), in an act of protest, and demand they take (good) care of it.
☞ Lobby your council to turn that abandoned shop on your local high street into a Care Rewear Repair pop-up rather than leaving it destitute.

If this sounds quite daunting, don't worry; there will be more in later chapters on how to maximize the life of your clothes with manual skills and modern technology, and how to activate your-self as an individual and in your community.

YOUR SEWING KIT

Building your own sewing kit is pure joy: in fact, it's so delectable that I own several, each for different needs. I have a travel kit, made from a tiny customized beauty case, which contains the kinds of implements that I need either because I will be in a hurry or in an emergency.

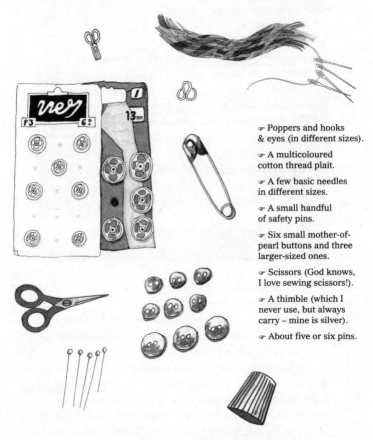

☞ Poppers and hooks & eyes (in different sizes).

☞ A multicoloured cotton thread plait.

☞ A few basic needles in different sizes.

☞ A small handful of safety pins.

☞ Six small mother-of-pearl buttons and three larger-sized ones.

☞ Scissors (God knows, I love sewing scissors!).

☞ A thimble (which I never use, but always carry – mine is silver).

☞ About five or six pins.

My stay-at-home kits are again made with repurposed objects (although a good friend gave me a classic Liberty's sewing kit and, I must admit, it's super-practical) and are classified by use: I have one mainly for darning and crochet; one for embellishing, containing a lifetime's worth of collected bits and pieces; and one for big jobs, with a metre rule, large scissors, lots of pins, chalks to mark stuff, and so on.

MY BADGES OF PRIDE

Photograph: Anna Stokland

☞ I collect vintage brooches, badges and pins, which I use to cover moth holes. It all started when one of my favourite jacket's lapels got attacked, and I covered the holes with every pin I had at my disposal. The final look was totally punk, and the jacket is one of my most admired pieces; I have been photographed wearing it several times. Everybody comments on the pins and brooches, unaware of the secret they are there to hide. Over the years I have extended this practice to knitwear and trousers too, and I never leave home without a few badges or pins in my bag, in case I spot a stain I can't get rid of with a quick on-the-go spongeing, or an unruly hole appears, which I don't like the look of. ✌

'CLOTHES AREN'T GOING TO

Anne Klein,

SAVE THE WORLD,

fashion designer

THE WOMEN WHO WEAR THEM WILL.'

STITCHING THE WORLD TOGETHER

There is another aspect of mending and circular thinking that is fundamental if we want to look at things differently, and that's the fact that to repair is native to humankind everywhere and, as such, it could provide us with the kind of cultural diversity that is so lacking in the fashion industry today.

Things in fashion work pretty much as 'West does it best', and we still operate much of the industry using the same parameters that rich Western nations used during colonial times: our aesthetic is the one that sells; thin white women are the best models; our style is better than yours . . . Well, not when it comes to mending and repairing. We all did it, and we all did it beautifully, and we all did it differently. Like all our heritage crafts (and we will look at this topic in Chapter 3), our mending techniques speak of our geographical circumstances – and so we could learn from each other, quite literally, one stitch at a time. The concept is the same – to prolong, to reinvent – but global regional variations in style and materials provide the nuances that make all mending techniques unique.

A few years ago I wrote this for the second Fashion Revolution Fanzine (also titled 'Loved Clothes Last'), and it still speaks of my feelings today:

> 'Mending doesn't mean we can't afford to buy something new, it means we can't afford something being thrown away. What used to be a badge of shame is now something to be proud of. Repairing our clothes is a practical, symbolic, aesthetic, original, creative, trendsetting, badass, revolutionary way to say my clothes are me, my chosen skin, my principles, my story. Long live my clothes!'

Chapter 3

Look Back
to Move Forward

Just like languages, crafts have been travelling, merging, changing, borrowing and lending, influencing and uniting people – our first transatlantic industry; but because they are so inextricably linked with our idea of history, it is hard to imagine them as anything other than a portal to our past, when in fact, for millennia, they were the opening to the future: a testament to our ingenuity, our mobility, our creativity and our productivity, on all levels.

As we finally understand the impact that accelerated growth has had on Planet Earth, its people and its biodiversity, we long once again for the comfort of heritage and tradition, the human hand-print left on handmade objects, and a return to a more personal connection with the clothes and accessories we buy, looking for products that are made to last.

This re-embracing of the past is taking several shapes: from fashion designers incorporating traditional designs into their aesthetic, to a markedly increased interest in learning crafts, or returning to them.

Fashion is closely linked with its artisanal practices, and the erosion of local craft cultures is yet another loss, akin to the near-extinction of rhinos, bees, polar bears and countless other creatures that have already been wiped off the face of Earth as we hit the most dramatic extinction rate of the past ten million years. So as well as our biodiverse ecosystem, we also stand to lose the diverse skills, crafts and heritage that human beings have spent millennia cultivating.

Ours is a case of spectacular self-harm, destroying civility in the name of civilization and eradicating ancient traditions, many of which are crucial in procuring abundance and prosperity for their local communities – all in the name of progress.

CRAFTING AS THE OG (ORIGINAL GANGSTER) INDUSTRY

The craft industry is as old as it is huge; the craft market was estimated to be worth around US $500 billion in 2017 and is expected to grow to more than $900 billion by 2023; and yet UNESCO estimates that more than 200 crafts from 100 countries are either already extinct or at risk of extinction, due to ongoing globalization.

In many ways, making things with our own two hands – crafting – is one of the most important qualities that make humans different from other animal species. Of course, all animals make things, but humans make with intention and imagination. Karl Marx wrote in *Das Kapital*, Volume 1, Chapter 7, 'A spider conducts operations that resemble those of a weaver, and a bee puts to shame many an architect in the construction of her cells. But what distinguishes the worst architect from the best of bees is this, that the architect raises his structure in imagination before he erects it in reality.'

Before the onset of the Industrial Revolution, all goods were made by hand. Sure, as our human ingeniousness progressed, so did our tools, but ultimately everything was handmade, the fruit of our geo-local cultures, folklore and handed-down wisdoms, with each region excelling and differing from the next. The exquisiteness of the lace from Burano may seem unparalleled until you see the wonders produced in the north of France, and Mexican embroidery arguably rivals in beauty anything stitched in the Middle East.

In that sense, I like to think of crafts as myths and fairy tales or regional food recipes, born and developed according to their unique local circumstances, with local ingredients and conditions dictating pretty much everything, from the type of wood or metal used to make tools and implements (which in turn affects the gauge and weave of a fabric), to the kind of fibre or material that is available; even natural dyes and colours are likely to differ from place to place, according to the weather, water and soil.

The whole world becomes a delicious minestrone soup when you look at crafts in this way: splashes of colour from far-away places, like the yellows from India or Naples; rough woollen textures from the North meeting fine silk weaves from the East; patterns and symbols repeated and reinterpreted according to different global points of view; skills perfected by thousands of different hands bringing their own intervention; secrets passed on and on, throughout generations and populations.

When I was a child we used to go on holiday a couple of hours north of Venice, in the South Tyrol region on the border with Austria, and the embroidered edelweiss was a recurring motif on every piece of cloth imaginable, from local dresses to kitchen towels. All local souvenirs, which at the time were made by local artisans and not mass-produced in China as they tend to be right now, were edelweiss-dependent. Many years later, travelling in Thailand in the late 1980s with my then three-year-old daughter, we visited a fairly secluded hill community. I was amazed to find imagery of that very familiar edelweiss nestled in very unfamiliar territory. Not completely identical, embroidered in a slightly different style and size, and proudly cohabiting with a totally different set of symbols and motifs from the ones in my memories, but unmistakably edelweiss. At first I was incredulous – it was just like meeting an old friend in the most unexpected of places – but then I connected all the dots and arrived at Marco Polo, probably the most famous Venetian of all time.

By the mid- to late 1200s Venice had established itself as the gateway to the East, connected all the way to China via the Silk Road, one of the world's earliest trade routes. It follows that cloth fabricated near Venice would have travelled and subsequently merged with textiles being made on the other side of the planet. There are lots of stories such as this one, and several symbols and patterns that pop up, like unexpected but welcome guests, from one culture to the other, spanning all the way from Nepal to Mexico, showing us the threads that connect us, the history of our travels and migrations.

Equally, some crafts were born spontaneously and simultaneously across the globe, testifying to the saying that 'great minds think alike' – an interesting phenomenon perfectly illustrated by the indigo plant. Indigo is a plant that grows, in different shapes and forms, all over the world, and although indigo dyeing was presumed to have originated in India (hence the plant's name), more recent archaeological finds point to a wider, localized use, from South America to the East, long before trade routes had been established – a brilliant example of isolated populations coming up with similar solutions, despite being thousands of miles apart.

FROM SUBSTANCE TO SPEED

Today, as a result of recent macro-trends like fast fashion and fast luxury, artisans are rapidly disappearing from the overall picture. After decades of quantity over quality, of idolizing perfection over the subtlety, intimacy and vulnerability of the handmade, our aesthetics have changed and we have become removed from the people who make our clothes; and there just aren't many people left who make things like they used to. We have stopped valuing this kind of work because we no longer see it happening around us.

Up until the late 1980s even major industrialized Western metropolises were awash with makers – from shoemakers to potters – and most people knew of (and used) the services of proficient local seamstresses to repair and alter or make from scratch something special. Nowadays these skilled makers are few and far between and needing all of our support.

I have been familiar with the doom of disappearing artisanal practices since I was small, as my mother reminded me of this likelihood each time we visited the glassblowers in Murano when I was a child. She'd say to me that she feared their craft wouldn't last, as a result of cheap, mass-produced glassware. She was right. I watched in dismay as, throughout my lifetime, first there were few, then fewer, then none. As a result, I try to keep alive as many other makers as I can, with my custom. It's about those objects that really matter, and spending money where a little more really makes a difference. An example would be my sketchbooks and diaries, which I buy (and have always bought) on a yearly basis from my favourite bookbinder in Venice, near the Frari Church. Yes, they are expensive, but considering how often I use them (daily) and how long for (one year for a diary, more for the sketchbooks), the heftier price brings with it a double guarantee: my product is of exquisite quality, and the bookbinder in Venice is still in existence. I always buy from skilled craftspeople if I want a very special gift – say, for a wedding or an anniversary.

The shift towards glamorizing glossy, unoriginal, mass-produced brands as opposed to artisanal and human-made products was probably also driven by the cyclical nature of fashion, and how trends tend to skip a couple of generations before being reclaimed as the latest thing. Nothing is truly new any more. The cut of our trousers is one of the best examples of this visual see-saw, going from skinny to flared, then back to skinny again several times throughout the 20th century. In fashion theory, this is often described as the pendulum swing of trends, meaning that a style – be it skirt length, trouser width or sleeve volume – swings from one pole to another. Once the style reaches its utmost extreme (think miniskirt, bell-bottom or mutton sleeve), it begins to move in the opposite direction.

It was during one of these transitions that we parked the 'ethnic look' in the archive at some point in the 1980s, following the hippy craze of the 1970s, where everything had a hint of Afghan embroidery to it. Yet the decline in handicrafts also coincides with the migration of the fashion industry towards developing countries, the onset of fast fashion and globalization, and it looks as if, in our search for cheaper and faster, we severely damaged millennia of hand-making traditions.

Importantly, the disregard and devaluation of ancient crafts and cultural artisan practices did not occur in isolation. The attitudes that we've ascribed to handmade objects follow a pattern of colonialism and 'othering' that Western nations have ascribed to cultures around the globe. When you consider how colonial controls have oppressed craft and culture, it is no wonder that indigenous crafts struggle to survive today. As we strive to make fashion more inclusive, celebrating and making amends to those once oppressed, it is important that we apply the same sensitivity to the forgotten crafts that were once so intrinsic to oppressed cultures.

For years now we have been led to believe that most handicrafts were not that interesting, a bit dull, a bit too 'ethnic', as if implying that ethnicity also meant slightly unpolished: a protracted stigma that has negatively affected many skilled artisans and was subsequently suffered by the first so-called 'eco-fashion' brands, as many of those pioneering labels were born out of a craving to preserve, support and commercialize the work of crafts-skilled marginalized communities.

I mostly blame the luxury sector for this visual bastardization, but at some point over the past 40 years we got confused between real luxury and mass-produced premium products; we started to believe in the shine and not the substance, in designer logos over human hand-print, worshipping the names of a few, over the wisdoms of the many. (We will touch upon the opposite of this, cultural appropriation – when brands appropriate indigenous or traditional crafts to follow a momentary trend – in Chapter 8.)

To me, real luxury isn't about serialized bags in fuchsia-pink suede produced in a factory somewhere in their millions and costing thousands; my real luxury will forever be the drop of blood on a hemline, reminding me that a person, with real life flowing through their fingers, was hand-sewing the piece that I coveted enough to own.

THE INTERNET AND THE RISE OF CRAFTIVISM

Today the Internet and social media have been a catalyst for crafters and makers worldwide, creating new opportunities to learn, showcase, sell and connect. Knowledge transfer occurs at the click of a button. Type whatever into your search engine, press Enter and there you are – only one step away from your desk and into any reality you wish to discover. It has never been easier to share, and makers the world over have been utilizing this visibility to learn from each other as well as to sell their wares, ensuring that artisanal techniques remain relevant. There are millions of online conversations happening right this minute about yarns, sewing, crochet and knitting, tatting and pattern-cutting. In 2019 the international social networking site for knitters and crocheters – Ravelry.com – boasted eight million members and growing.

When it comes to a blueprint for a future fashion industry, one where monopolies are limited and original creativity and innovation are celebrated, supported and replicated, there is nothing more modern than the history and the development of artisanal skills and artisanal products. Crafts were the original open-source, which is why I find it so inspiring that with the rise of the Internet we have also seen the rise of a huge community dedicated to making, with the World Wide Web providing ways to revive skills and embed them in entirely new systems.

The Internet has also facilitated crafts to become a symbol of protest. In January 2017, as more than four million people participated in women's marches around the globe to protest at the inauguration of a misogynistic American president, handmade pussy hats from an open-source crochet pattern became the international symbol of opposition.

Activism – which evokes a loud, crowded and often draining form of resistance – has been subverted by the maker movement in the advent of *craftivism*. The term was introduced by the maker and writer Betsy Greer at the beginning of the millennium, and was later championed by the activist Sarah Corbett as a movement of its own – and as the introvert's agent of change. Craftivism affects change first by subverting the 'domestic arts', long relegated to the home and dismissed as 'women's work'. It takes a quieter, more personal approach to activism. Occasionally the concept has been employed for specific and goal-orientated campaigns, such as in 2015 when Corbett and her Craftivist Collective used embroidered, handmade handkerchiefs to successfully lobby for a living wage at one of the UK's largest retailers. It doesn't need to be that pointed, though. Journalist Jake Hall writes of craftivism in the fourth Fashion Revolution Fanzine:

'TAKING THE TIME TO MAKE SOMETHING FROM NOTHING IS A POLITICAL ACT IN A WORLD DRIVEN BY OVERCONSUMPTION.'

This is incredibly powerful. I believe there is a cosmic energy, an invisible thread that telepathically connects us as we simultaneously channel similar thoughts, and millions of people united in making are the perfect example of what needs to happen now: a gargantuan amplification of positive thoughts that lead to positive actions. In my opinion, makers are the modern-day heroes, the guardians of an important legacy: in an industry that produces hundreds of billions of garments every year, those advocating and practising a conscious slowdown are the ones pioneering change, using needles and social-media platforms as tools to fight this modern illness.

DEMOCRATIC FASHION AND PATTERNS FOR CHANGE

People talk about fast fashion as a democratization of fashion, regarding its affordability and ready availability as a sign of inclusiveness. However, nothing that is born of exploitation and misery can ever be described as democratic or inclusive – democracy and inclusivity cannot extend solely to the final users, but should be equally distributed throughout the supply chain. But when we look at the history of home-sewing and domestic crafts, and in particular that of ready-made, multi-sized paper patterns, which date back to 1863 when Ellen Butterick and her tailor husband Ebenezer founded the Butterick Company, we can see glimpses of a fashion that was designed for sharing; a fashion that encouraged individualism while setting its own trends, where it was possible to intervene as an individual on a product shared by the masses. All sewing patterns of the same design may be identical, but each piece made will reflect the individual choices of the maker: their size, shape, fabric preferences and personal embellishments. It was truly democratic, it was readily available and it levelled out the playing field: if you could sew, you could look as polished as anyone with money, for a fraction of the price.

My daughter Elisalex – founder of the sewing-pattern label By Hand London; a sewist, teacher and influencer among the maker community – wrote in the *Surface Design* journal:

By the early 1900s, the sewing pattern market was booming. New companies such as Vogue Patterns, Simplicity, DuBarry and Advance were cropping up well into the 1930s, with most of them advertising their patterns . . . with their own magazines. Sewing machines had become more affordable and widely owned throughout North America and Europe, but so had mass-produced fashion thanks to the industrialization of the clothing industry. It is fair to suggest that the initial cachet that home sewing offered following Singer's innovation and the first sewing patterns (specifically designed to offer American women the opportunity to replicate exclusive French fashions), began to wane as affordable commercial fashion became more readily available, and economic slumps such as The Great Depression and the Second World War meant that, once again, the only women making their own clothes were the ones who could not afford to buy new.

Interestingly, it was the advance of the internet, and specifically "blogging" in the very early 2000s, that catalysed the resurgence in home sewing . . . Blogs gave individuals a platform to share their hobbies, learn from others, and connect with like-minded people. In this way, underground trends – like sewing, and other analogue hobbies also growing in popularity as a means to balance out an increasingly fast paced and digital existence – were able to spread quickly and reach more and more people the world over. Sewing blogs provided women (and some men!) with a sense of community that encouraged the expression of personal style and the freedom of being able to make and wear clothes that fit well.'

With the onset of the Internet, and as a reaction to cheap fashion's design uniformity, demand for this kind of service has greatly increased: it is estimated that in 2014, in the UK alone, 3.5 million people made their own clothes, and more than 430,000 of them had only started learning how to sew the previous year. This number has palpably kept on growing ever since, and we can now search for a myriad of ways to learn and share, as well as look online to find classes and events in person, which are very much on the increase.

LEARN TO SEW . . .
BUT WHERE TO BEGIN?

☞ **Visit your local haberdashery**: Despite a steady decline in traditional haberdasheries on our high streets, we are seeing a new crop of trendy, independent crafting retailers and crafting cafés dotted all over the world, usually staffed by enthusiastic makers who will be more than happy to get you started with the basic kit and a generous dose of infectious inspiration!

☞ **Attend a sewing class**: Dive right in, pick your teacher's brain and make some new like-minded sewing friends along the way.

☞ **Seek out sewing blogs**: Search for posts like 'sewing tips for beginners' and you'll discover a whole world of people who spend their free time creating free content for people who love to make stuff.

☞ **Watch YouTube**: Search for clear and easy-to-follow video tutorials that will teach you everything from sewing your first seam to constructing a zip fly.

☞ **Find your community**: Join the inspiring, friendly and welcoming online sewing community on Instagram. Follow hashtags like #sewcialists, #sewersofinstagram and #imade-myclothes to discover, connect and share your journey.

I see the phenomenon of crafting online (and offline) as a weapon for mass education, a revolutionary citizens' engagement in making things, with meaning. Whether you want to try your hand at sewing, knitting, crochet, embroidery, quilting, pottery, shoemaking, weaving, macramé or natural dyeing, there is no shortage of crafts waiting to be rediscovered.

During times of social and political unrest, a lot can be said with crafts, and although we may not be able, as individuals, to turn the tide of climate heating one knitting needle at a time, we can use crafts in conjunction with advocacy as a template for our personal participation in a process of climate action.

RELAXATION
AND REVOLUTION

Reclaiming traditions and handicraft skills is the perfect antidote to today's accelerated rhythm; and another aspect of sewing, knitting, crocheting, embroidering and making that we have forgotten to love is the mindful relaxation and sense of well-being that comes with it.

Crafting often brings with it a sense of being immersed in the moment – soothing gestures that bring the physical contentment that comes from owning a lovely end product, the pride of having made it, and the abstraction of thoughts that occurs when undertaking this kind of manual work. Basically: bliss. And this blissed-out state is scientifically proven to have positive effects on our health, as it is linked with the release of dopamine and serotonin, naturally occurring hormones that can improve our mood as well as acting as a mild painkiller.

Craft courses have been prescribed to patients since the dawn of occupational therapy in the late 19th century, with basketry used to relieve anxiety and physical ailments among soldiers during the First World War. 'Cultural activities encourage gentle movement, reduce social isolation, and lower inflammation and stress hormones such as cortisol,' says Dr Daisy Fancourt of the UK Crafts Council. 'The arts are linked with dopamine release, which encourages cognitive flexibility, and they reduce our risk of dementia.'

In short, there's a lot to be said for gentle, repetitive movements and their effect on our mental sanity: think about babies being rocked to sleep, or the act of pacing a room when nervous, or tapping and shaking legs and fingers, or fidgeting in general. It's soothing, it's *rhythmical*, predictable and reassuring. People do it instinctively to stay calm and to aid concentration – a primeval form of physical meditation.

'Open attention to and awareness of the clothes in our wardrobe, like that which occurs as we mend, offers the prospect of a changed relationship with fashion consumption. It works with a similar mechanism of influence as mindfulness and its attention to the

present moment, to savouring experience, which
in turn reduces desire for external pleasures that
depend on money and material goods. Psychological
studies suggest that a capacity for mindfulness – that
is, attention to and awareness of internal states and
external events in the present moment – results in less
emphasis being placed on materialistic values, like
image, and greater emphasis on internal aspirations,
such as community involvement and personal
development, that don't require major material inputs.'

Kate Fletcher, *The Craft of Use: Post-Growth Fashion*, 2016

The truth is that those who make will find time for making, because making makes you feel good. Furthermore, if you think about it, most activities like sewing, crocheting and knitting are physically and mentally not that dissimilar to playing video games on our phones or iPads, requiring the same kind of gentle hand-motions, precision, repetition, obsession and a temporary distance from the outside world – which is why it is so important that we strengthen their role in our kids' education, in school curricula and after-school activities, from which they are decreasing year after year, due to cuts and lack of funding: the challenge lies in making them as appealing as scrolling on Instagram.

Interestingly, in early-1800s Britain, when middle-class families had cultural aspirations for their daughters in order to better themselves in society, women who spent too much time embroidering for their own pleasure would have been criticized for much the same reasons that we scold our kids today for spending too much time in front of their computer screens or phones (just as I would have been scolded, as a child, for spending too much time in front of the TV). Excessive embroidery was considered frivolous and quite unhealthy, as it required too many hours sitting down, and too much inner-focused concentration. Much better to spend time reading or outside in the fresh air!

As any maker will agree, needlework and yarn crafts can be an addiction in themselves, albeit ones that yield something incredibly precious at the end. Unlike *Tetris*. Or *Candy Crush*.

I WAS A MAKER

My whole career in fashion started with a hole, a crochet needle, some beads and a ball of yarn, in 1997. My Venetian grandmother, Nonna Stanilla, taught me how to crochet when I was six and, as far as I am concerned, not even learning how to drive several years later compares to the high of being capable of essentially creating fabric.

Even then, I was aware that to be able to make cloth was going to be as vital for my existence as it had been vital for my ancestors and, indeed, humankind, because of both its creative and its practical potential. I had wild images of being lost in the woods and using my yarn and my needle for survival and protection.

One day in early 1997 I was invited to the Turner Prize Gala Dinner, and it was one of those 'I Have Nothing to Wear' days (despite two wardrobes being full). The thing was that I really wanted to wear my then-favourite cardigan, an orange Benetton one that I had been carrying around with me for a good 15 years already, and which was by then covered in holes – elbows gone, several small moth holes at the front and one wrist completely frayed. At the time, despite being at the height of grunge, holes weren't acceptable, not at the Turner Prize Gala Dinner anyway. And so I was left with no choice: mend the jumper or show up in something I didn't really want to wear.

I took my thinnest crochet needle (0.75mm) and started to delicately crochet around all the holes, so as not to disturb them, but instead to emphasize them, make them the centre of my jumper-world. Some of them I left quite plain (the smaller ones), while on others I continued with the crochet and created a chain-stitch around them, to make the hole look like a small flower. On the vast expanse of elbow holes I added some weight by threading beads on my yarn, before crocheting around them.

By the end of the evening I had amassed many private orders, all from people who had some story or other concerning their favourite jumper having been discarded because of moths or general wear-and-tear; and within a short space of time I went from mending a few pieces to selling jumpers with crochet holes internationally in some of the best boutiques in London, New York, Milan and Tokyo, and being worn by many cool celebrities of the 1990s.

Within one year of starting my business I was employing 14 women to crochet, and was buying cashmere jumpers by the tonne, turning a simple act of care into a career. With my brand, From Somewhere, and my husband, Filippo, we went on to reuse tonnes of pre- and post-consumer surplus and waste, sold internationally in some of the world's best boutiques, as well as designing and producing upcycled collections with Jigsaw, Robe di Kappa, Tesco Clothing, Speedo and Topshop. We closed in 2014; long live From Somewhere!

To this day I am never too far from a thin crochet needle and a ball of mercerized cotton yarn; from quickly creating a delicate motif to use in case I have a stain to cover up, or a hair accessory to customize, to crocheting on borders to add something more to a plain cardigan or long-sleeved T-shirt. I once completely altered the drape of a silk jersey dress, which was too flimsy and inconsistent for my liking, by adding several rounds of crochet as a trim at the hemline; it fell beautifully with the added weight.

We often consider 'investment buying' (as in buying something more expensive, which by implication we consider to be better made and destined to last longer) as the only contrast to buying cheaply. Well, there is no better way to 'invest' than to make it yourself: investing your time, investing your thoughts and investing your creativity to make something from scratch, or to mend something broken.

Chapter 4

Why Care?

When we think about washing our clothes we tend to think no further than the job at hand: dirty clothes, washing machine, tumble dry, done. In actual fact the daily care of our clothing has a huge impact on the planet, and if we took a little bit more time to change our habits and wash with real care, we would be drastically reducing our carbon footprint, as well as protecting our oceans and, ultimately, all living species on Earth.

Washing uses water, this miraculous living substance of which we still know so little, and the water that we use every day is the same water that has been used every day since the very beginning – and will continue to be used every day – until for ever. Water regenerates and is continuously recycled, but it is always the same water. When it rains, that's not new water that is formed in the clouds, but the very same water that we pumped out of our washing machines, the same water we used in the shower, the same water we contaminate with toxic chemicals in the making and caring for our clothes. It runs in (dead) rivers, it reaches our (polluted) oceans, it evaporates into the sky and it rains back down upon us, containing all the same indelible ingredients we contaminated it with.

This is why debris from our insatiable appetite for polyester (this debris is known as microfibres, more on those later) has been found not just at the bottom of our deepest oceans, but all the way at the top of Mount Everest as well. Microfibres rained on London recently, and were found in the spray from the waves during a thunderstorm. When we think of our polluted waterways we assume that the culprits are factories, or agriculture, but it is also us, every single day, with every single wash, consistently, relentlessly releasing toxicants into the system.

So when a statistic says that in order to produce a cotton T-shirt we use 2,700 litres of water, that doesn't mean that the water is lost because we have used it up; it is in fact much, much worse than that: it means that 2,700 litres of water have been spoiled, contaminated and poisoned. If that same T-shirt had been produced without the use of fertilizers, pesticides and toxic dyes, the problem wouldn't exist.

We contribute to this insane intoxication every time we wash our clothes, which is why we need to understand that clothing care is no longer just a personal household duty, but a collective duty for the future health of our planet.

LONGEVITY MATTERS

The advent of the electric washing machine in 1908 created a distance between our hands and our dirty clothes – a distance that has become a gulf over the years. We simply do not know our stains any more, because we don't spend hours trying to rub them out. We can't understand why a jumper shrinks because we can't see it happening before our very eyes. Above all, because washing machines have made washing our clothes so very easy, we pump them full of clothes at the very first sight of dirt, real or pre-empted. When clothes washing was done by hand, it was a real hassle, it was exhausting, it ruined your hands and required enormous strength – think of all that wringing and hanging out to dry – so it is no surprise that women (as washing was exclusively women's work, after all) invented so many ways to delay washing until absolutely necessary. Spot-cleaning, brushing and refreshing were all quick-fix solutions that saved time, effort and money. Nowadays it is the opposite: shoving a pile of laundry in the wash is far more convenient and efficient than paying individual attention to each little stain that appears throughout the week.

But let's stop for a moment and try to compromise between what is convenient for us and what is convenient for our environment: a quick clothes scan is all you need to check how much your laundry is selfish or selfless. By using the information at hand, understanding the properties of the materials our clothes are made of and the care-labels we are provided with, we can put our clothing to better use and wear it much longer, and if we can double the useful lifespan of our clothes, we can reduce their carbon footprint by 24 per cent.

Once again I look at food as an example. When we buy food, one of the first things we check before buying is the sell-by date: we know that certain products will have to be rigorously kept in the fridge (meat, fish, dairy), while others (vegetables, for instance) can be stored in a cupboard. We store our food according to a set of universal instructions, some of which are spelled out for us on labels and some that are ingrained in us from childhood: you wouldn't put a packet of biscuits in the fridge, but you would refrigerate a cake to keep it fresh for longer. Next we scan the ingredients: does it contain gluten, or harmful colourants, or too much sugar? Well, the clothes we wear have ingredients and a sell-by date too. We just need to learn how to read them.

The truth is that although we have retained some innate knowledge about the way we wash our clothes – like the fact that cotton whites will be whiter if washed at a high temperature, while wool on the other hand needs to be washed at a low temperature to prevent it from shrinking – we seldom play or interact with that knowledge, we don't put it to good enough use, and more often than not we don't understand the attributes that make each fabric unique.

Clothing was designed to be worn for years (with disposal only intended to occur at the point of disintegration beyond repair), while most current washing techniques are about making clothes look or smell better, not about making them last longer or keeping tabs on the way they impact upon the environment. To make a difference, longevity and environmental impact have to be the priority when we're caring for our clothes, with improved aesthetics a happy by-product.

When it comes to caring for our clothes, machines have certainly made the whole process infinitely easier, although modern washing is not necessarily better for the health of our clothes, or the health of our planet. Today's machines are actually quite vicious in their cycles, especially if coupled with the detergents that are on the market, which are also designed to be quite aggressive on the fabrics they are supposed to clean. This is because the combination of machine plus detergent is there to substitute the hard graft and attention to detail that came with centuries of hand-washing, intense scrubbing, sinking and hand-wringing.

Above all we must be careful to use our machines efficiently, avoid washing when something isn't actually dirty, and be mindful of the amount of detergent we use. I promise you that one tablespoon of powdered clothing detergent is all that you need for a good clean, and that washing everyday stuff at a lower heat doesn't make much of a difference to the overall cleanliness of your load. I avoid fabric softener like the plague, as I detest that fuzzy feeling of fake chemical softness, but I do add a few drops of lavender oil (or any other oil that takes my fancy) to my bedsheets and towels wash.

UNDERSTANDING + LEARNING TO READ CARE SYMBOLS

1. Machine washable
2. Synthetics cycle
3. Gentle/wool wash cycle
4. Hand-wash
5. Do not wash
6. Do not wring
7. Wash max 30°
8. Wash max 40°
9. Wash max 60°
10. Iron allowed
11. Iron low temperature
12. Iron medium temperature
13. Iron high temperature
14. Do not iron
15. Do not steam
16. Tumble dry allowed
17. Tumble dry low heat
18. Tumble dry medium heat
19. Tumble dry high heat
20. Permanent press
21. Delicate/gentle
22. No heat
23. Do not tumble dry
24. Hang to dry
25. Drip dry
26. Dry flat
27. Dry in the shade
28. Dry clean only
29. Do not dry clean
30. Any solvent
31. Any solvent except tetrachloroethene
32. Petroleum solvent only
33. Bleaching allowed
34. Use non-chlorine bleach
35. Do not bleach

I read recently in *The Guardian* that a low-heat wash (at 30 degrees Celsius), which is hung on the line and not tumble dried, will release 0.6 kg of CO_2. This figure rises to 0.7 if washing at 40 degrees, but increases exponentially if the washing cycle is combined with tumble drying: up to 2.4 kg of CO_2 if using a vented dryer, and a whopping 3.3 kg in a combined washer-dryer.

And this is the damage we do to our environment via energy use. The damage to our clothing isn't measurable, but it is visible over time – jumpers pull, colours fade, shapes are lost, fabrics are weakened.

As every fabric reacts differently to wear, to water, to heat, to rinsing and spinning, each with its own unique preferences, knowing what our clothes are made of is the key to unlocking how we care for them and make them last, as well as the start of a journey towards a better understanding of the effect their materials have on our environment – principally on our soil and water. So just as it is important to remember that wool shrinks when washed hot, or that linen wants to stay creased even under the hottest iron, we need to know that most synthetic fibres were designed to perform better than their natural counterparts, in particular around issues of durability and care, and require a different kind of maintenance.

#WHATSINMYCLOTHES?

The properties of the fibres are the visible ingredients – the cloth – but what about the hidden ones: the chemicals used to make that cloth, the treatments it underwent, the dyes it takes its colour from?

Our skin is the second most absorbing organ in our body, and the clothes we buy, especially when we have just bought them, are full of toxic substances, from dyes to fixatives and fire retardants. We know that some dyes are more harmful than others: black dye in particular has been linked to several types of health issues (certain cancers and endocrine conditions) and yet do you bother to wash your brand-new black jeans, or your black underwear, before you wear it? Probably not. And even if you did, are you aware of what you are sharing with everyone else, via your seemingly innocent wash?

We probably wouldn't be so carefree around our clothing if we really knew what's lurking inside it . . . I will talk extensively about transparency and traceability (or the lack thereof) in Chapter 9, but this is a fundamental issue: unlike other industries, which are regulated, such as food and pharmaceuticals, the fashion industry is not, meaning that transparency, public disclosure and traceability of products from raw materials to manufacturing are not mandatory. This in turn means there are no legal obligations for brands to give us credible and comparable information on the products we buy, where they were made, by whom, utilizing what materials and under what circumstances, which leaves us with a great big gaping hole when it comes to finding out more.

In a recent chemical analysis undertaken by Buzzi Lab in Prato, Italy, it was discovered that a substantial percentage of cheap clothing made in countries such as China and Bangladesh still contains toxicants that have already been banned in the EU, and many do not give an accurate list of the materials being used. It may say '10 per cent cashmere' on the label, but on closer analysis there may actually be no cashmere whatsoever under the microscope – so when it comes to taking responsibility for our clothes and how we consume and care for them, we have to do the detective work ourselves. If we don't know what's in our clothes, how can we possibly know how to care for them?

Toxic dyes are a very real and very invisible problem, when it comes to fashion and accessories, not least because it is estimated that 20 per cent of all water contamination is a direct result of the dyeing and treating of textiles – there is a popular saying in China that you can predict the next 'it' colour just by looking at the rivers.

Of course, deadly shades are nothing new, and throughout history we have been misusing toxic chemicals (inhaling them, plastering them on our bodies and using them in our surroundings) in the name of the perfect colour tone. White lead, one of the most poisonous substances, was used as foundation for centuries, and most famously by Queen Elizabeth I. Orpiment, a dusty yellow pigment brewed from arsenic and sulphide, was long known as the 'King's Gold'. Scheele's Green is perhaps the most tragic example of how we compromised our well-being to look good. Made from copper arsenic, Scheele's Green was used to colour artificial flower leaves and lime-coloured gowns. For those who wore it and worked with it, the toxic pigment left fingernails and the whites of eyes the same acidic shade of green.

Yet evolution should be about learning from past mistakes in order to become better, and in our case we are doing precisely the opposite: we know the risks and we keep taking them. Our clothes are teeming with toxicants, some of which have long been banned from the food industry as they are deemed too dangerous to ingest, and yet not only are we wearing them against our absorbent skin, but the fact that these dyes and toxicants are released into public waterways even after repeated washes implies that our judgement, when it comes to absorption and contamination, is precarious to say the least.

A modern-day example is azo dyes, which are used to make bright, fluorescent and permanent shades, due to their increased fastness (that is, they don't discolour after washing). These dyes are very widely in use, both by the fast-fashion and the luxury sector; and as recent research on the ScienceDirect website shows, they have been classified as carcinogenic if affected by light, temperature, pH changes and water – meaning that we absorb them and release them in public waterways with repeated use. The risks are also extended to workers making our clothes throughout the supply chain, and their working environment. Some azo dyes have been banned in Europe since 2002, but many are, crucially, still in use in the textile industry.

International laws, such as the California Proposition 65, are increasingly providing information on the effects of toxicants for factory workers and citizens, and the usage of some azo dyes is now banned in China, Japan, India and Vietnam; but without mandatory transparency, full public disclosure and regulations, open borders and online selling make it virtually impossible to know what's in our clothes, as we cannot necessarily trust the labels.

Dyeing things differently

In the near future we will look at textile colourants differently. What constitutes the 'perfect pink' today? Some like it hot, others go for candy or pastel, but the perfect pink of tomorrow is one that hasn't been drenched in harmful treatments, whose waters were recycled, and which doesn't contain azo dyes and other toxicants. In fact, the perfect shade of millennial pink can be created at home using another millennial staple: the avocado.

HOW TO DYE FABRIC BLUSH-PINK WITH AN AVOCADO

☞ Start by prepping your fabric for the dye-bath. You'll want to be using natural fibres like cotton, silk or linen: give it a good soak so that it's damp before it goes in the dye. You can pre-treat the fabric with a 'mordant', which is a fixative that helps the dye to stay put, or you can dunk the fabric in salt water after the dye-bath, which does pretty much the same thing. ✂

☞ Fill a big pot with water and clean avocado skins, stones; simmer – do not boil – for about half an hour until you see the colour start to change. Stir the fabric into the pot and continue to simmer for an hour or two. ✂

☞ Turn off the heat, but leave the fabric to steep until you're happy with the colour: overnight is usually a good bet! ✂

☞ Rinse the fabric in cool salt water and hang to dry (away from direct sunlight, as this will affect the natural dye). ✂

YOUR REGULAR WASH

It's all about 'looking back to move forward', and repurposing old methods that may seem obsolete in today's lifestyle, but which carry a gentler footprint than our present reliance of shoving everything in our regular wash. Here are a few simple tips to make caring for your clothes an integrated part of your day-to-day routine.

STEAMING *(also in the shower)*

Steaming will immediately refresh a piece and release most of the creases, making it look more polished; plus it gets rid of odours, so for outerwear such as coats and jackets, for knitwear and more formal wear such as suits or evening wear, a quick turn in the shower is a lifesaver.

As for steaming machines, the portable ones are brilliant. They get rid of every crease imaginable, which is why they are so widely used in the fashion industry, from retailers to runway shows. Bonus point: the steam effectively disinfects clothing by killing up to 99 per cent of all bacteria.

☞ Turn the hot tap on, close the shower curtain or door and hang your garment as close as possible to the tap without it getting wet – on the rail or shower door is best, but anywhere in the bathroom will suffice.

☞ Close the bathroom door to keep the heat in and let the steam do its bit for a few minutes (keep checking that the clothes aren't being soaked!).

☞ I add essential oils on a little plate, which I leave close to the shower, but not on the floor or in direct contact with the water (my favourite oils are rose, bergamot and lavender; rosemary is good with odours too), but near enough that the heat will encourage the oils to diffuse.

HAND-WASHING *(in the bath and in the shower or the sink)*

Actually I don't hand-wash that often, but I know several people who do, and love it. I used to hand-wash all my knits, until I found that a good wool machine-wash at 20 degrees and drying flat (laying out my damp garment on a towel over a drying rack) was a better option for me. But I do wash my underwear by hand quite often, in the bath or in the shower, especially when I am travelling.

☞ As you shower, block the drain and allow the basin to fill (enough water to cover your feet is plenty). If you're bathing in a tub, retain some of the water instead of letting it all drain out. If you don't have a bath, and your shower is the flat kind that can't collect water, then the bathroom sink is a perfectly viable alternative.

☞ Add a little eco-detergent (or I use plain shower gel, if I'm in a hotel) to the water and give it a little froth-up with your hands.

☞ Let your underwear soak as you dry off and get yourself dressed.

☞ Manually scrub, rinse and hang your underwear over a radiator or drying rack. It will dry overnight, ready for wear again the next day!

This system works well for me, as I often really need to wash only three pairs of pants and a bra at a time; and if I urgently need them outside my regular, twice-weekly family wash, then I will wash them this way. When I travel, I do this religiously.

By washing gently by hand, my underwear spends less time bouncing around the washing machine, thereby reducing my contribution of microplastics and taking less of a toll on delicate lingerie fabrics such as silk and lace.

SPOT-CLEANING

My favourite technique by far; I literally carry a small sponge with me wherever I go, just in case. If you act fast, you can spot-clean using only your sponge and a bit of warm water, without detergent, although I will add a drop of apple cider vinegar if I have some. Stubborn stains, such as red wine, won't completely go away, but minor ones will, if you rub hard enough (best to rub following the grain of the fabric, so as to disturb it as little as possible). A clever tip: a dry sponge pressed hard onto a wet stain will absorb most of the stain's moisture, thereby containing it. When spot-cleaning at home I use a tiny bit of detergent, but only very, very little or the lather risks leaving a kind of halo effect on the fabric. On greasy stains I prefer to use clear dish-soap, or powder preferably, in minuscule amounts.

I really hate to say this, because I do not advocate the use of wet-wipes unless absolutely necessary, but the truth is that they de-stain brilliantly in an emergency. Just make sure that you only ever buy the most biodegradable wet-wipes you can find!

BRUSHING

If this is good enough for Stella McCartney (and, apparently, HRH The Prince of Wales), surely it must be worth taking into consideration?

Brushing works wonders with wools and tweeds. Because of the way the material is so tightly woven, stains often sit on the surface, without penetrating the fabric too deeply. A good brushing is often all that is needed to get rid of that mud, jam, honey or anything that gloops.

Wait until the offending gunk dries and use a clothes brush – one that has tightly packed natural bristles – to gently buff the stain away. Done deal.

FREEZING

This technique is a favourite among denim purists who go to seemingly extreme lengths to avoid actually washing their jeans (Levi's even provide a branded freezer bag with certain purchases): simply throw them in the freezer overnight and the lowered temperature will kill most odour-causing bacteria and refresh your garment. My main issue with this is that my freezer is always way too full to house my clothing at any given point. So either I freeze my clothes just after I empty it to defrost it (as one should do regularly, about once a year) – in which case I keep one day for freezing clothes before refilling it – or I clean out one drawer to use exclusively for this purpose. Truth be told, I am actually contemplating buying a small freezer to keep near my laundry so that I can practise this method on a more regular basis, because, especially for moths, it really does work.

As an absolutely brilliant anti-moth treatment, wash your knit-wear thoroughly and then freeze it overnight to kill the pesky moth larvae.

STAINS

For effective stain removal, certain ingredients are a must, and you should always have them to hand: salt (coarse or fine), vinegar, denatured alcohol and bicarbonate of soda.

Depending on the stain, salt is ideal for absorbing excess liquid while gently de-staining at the same time:

☞ Apply to stubborn wet stains immediately after spillage – think liquids such as red wine, tea and tomatoes.

☞ Leave to cover the stain for 20 minutes before scrubbing or soaking.

Vinegar, bicarbonate of soda and alcohol are powerful cleaning agents that you can add to your soak or regular machine-wash or use for spot-cleaning. When it comes to kids' clothes – particularly T-shirts, jeans and summer dresses – if I can't get rid of stubborn stains, I will get creative with them. Have you ever heard of 'pareidolia'? That's when you see shapes and faces on things like stones or clouds. It's such a fun game to play with kids, and with stained clothes!

You look at the stain and you see a shape in it, then you take fabric felt-tips or paints (or embroidery, if you're that good) and you bring that form to life. It could be an animal, a flower, a constellation or a monster. Those are the clothes you'll keep for ever, and the clothes your kids will want to wear again and again, because they contain their imagination and their own, unique intervention.

We need to control how we care for our clothes, we need to imagine their whole lifecycle, as soon as they become ours, and plan for their future before we include them in our lives. This is what this book is intended to help you do; it won't spoon-feed you many answers, but it will help you formulate a lot of questions, connecting your actions from the moment you buy something to the moment you get rid of it, so that you can act responsibly and with purpose.

Asking yourself some simple questions at the point of purchase is the best place to start:

☞ What materials is this piece made from? (Check the label before buying.)

☞ What are the cleaning recommendations? And do you really need another dry-clean-only sequinned number to wear at the office Christmas party? Does it have further use later on? If not, might you consider renting a glamorous outfit instead?

☞ Is it made of polyester? If so, is the poly used efficiently? Is it a piece that will require less care (because by now you know that polyester is a material that can be washed infrequently) or is it a T-shirt that will react badly to your natural body odour and therefore need frequent washing?

☞ Can you creatively imagine another use for the item you are about to buy? Like: *Ooooh, nice trousers! I can't wait to use them for a long time and then turn them into shorts!* Or: *Love this, but it might not be right for me if I gain/lose a few kilos, so who else in my life (mother/daughter/bff) might adopt it after me?*

Why care? Because something as banally simple as the way we wash our clothes is one of those steps we can all take right now to make small changes that aren't so hard to carry out after all. Understanding materials, where they come from and what they are made of is crucial to caring for our clothes better. Lavishing care and attention on the clothes we already own is not only personally fulfilling; understanding that the way we care for our clothes has a profound impact on the environment and, consequently, on climate change and global heating is fundamental to developing better washing habits – and sticking to them.

Chapter 5

Fabrics
of Our Lives

The Fashion Revolution Manifesto, which we launched in April 2018 during Fashion Revolution Week, is a vision for tomorrow, set in the present, and its point no. 6 says: 'Fashion conserves and restores the environment. It does not deplete precious resources, degrade our soil, pollute our air and water or harm our health. Fashion protects the welfare of all living things and safeguards our diverse ecosystems.'

Of course, this should be a mantra for all industries, and we certainly cannot lay the blame for exploitation of the planet and its living things exclusively at fashion's doorstep, but it is an industry of leaders and followers, as well as one of the most exploitative and polluting industries, so it has its fair share of responsibilities. Furthermore, as we all wear clothes, it has a massive potential to spearhead long-lasting, drastic improvements.

When it comes to the health of Mother Earth, we are at a very critical moment. From the biodiversity of our land and waters to the imminence of climate breakdown, the greatest threat to our collective future is our own human activity.

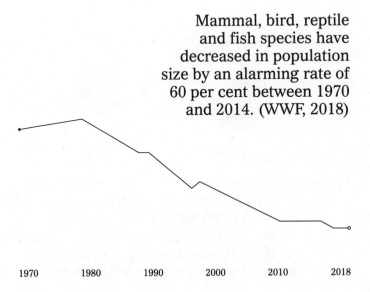

Mammal, bird, reptile and fish species have decreased in population size by an alarming rate of 60 per cent between 1970 and 2014. (WWF, 2018)

1970   1980   1990   2000   2010   2018

To make matters worse, even below the 2 degrees Celsius global-warming scenario that we are headed for, almost 25 per cent of species will be at risk of disappearing due to the impact of climate change on our ecosystems (WWF, 2018). As this catastrophic acceleration can be firmly linked to man-made activities, it looks as if pretty much everywhere we go, humans create damage, and our destruction is horrendously visible: deforestation, ice melting at unprecedented speed, the expansion of cities and endless suburbia, rampant industrialization. The age of the Anthropocene (the current human-centric geological era) has already left scars that can't be healed, and unless we remedy this, our planet will wither and so will all life on it. It's humans who did this, because humans were too cool to care.

We have been quite arrogant in our assumption that we are the most intelligent creatures on this planet, and in looking for other intelligent life forms in space; had we spent as much time and money on first understanding the Earth, on respecting, exploring and studying creatures more intelligent than (or as intelligent as) ourselves, we would be more in awe of our own planet and less inclined to destroy it.

40% of insect species under threat of extinction

20% of plants under threat of extinction

Over 40 per cent of insect species (according to Francisco Sánchez-Bayo and Kris A. G. Wyckhuys in 'Worldwide decline of the entomofauna', 2019) and 20 per cent of plants (Royal Botanic Gardens, Kew, 2016) are considered to be under threat of extinction.

FIBRES AS BUILDING BLOCKS

If we are to mitigate fashion's considerable negative impact on our planet, then the materials that comprise our wardrobe are a good place to start. Like the food industry, fashion's ingredients are the consequences of crop monocultures, harmful chemicals and the exploitation of precious non-renewable resources. So if we are to right the wrongs of our clothes' environmental transgressions, we must first learn to understand these raw materials, so that we can buy better, care better and encourage the fashion industry to write better recipes for better fabrics.

This chapter looks at fabrics by fibre type, meaning that the materials are categorized by their matter. Cotton, linen, polyester and rayon: these are all types of fibres that form synonymous fabrics. Of course, many materials today are blends of more than one fibre. Jeans (see Chapter 6) are often cotton blended with elastane for that figure-hugging stretch. Loungewear increasingly consists of polyester blended with cotton. And chunky-knit jumpers at high-street prices are usually acrylic or polyester, with an added bit of wool. We'll learn more about blended fibres in Chapter 7 but for now we'll take a look at the most prominent fabrics hanging in our wardrobes.

COTTON

A crop that was grown for millennia throughout the world, cotton reached northern Europe in the Middle Ages. Its German name, *Baumwolle*, means 'wool tree', and the story goes that people literally thought it came from a plant that produced baby lambs.

In her book *The Misinformation Age*, Cailin O'Connor writes about this persistent myth of the baby-lamb tree. To her, it represents our tendency to spread false facts, even when we're presented with tangible contrary evidence – the same people must have seen lambs being born by natural means. I bring this up because if we are to fix the broken fashion system, we must be able to overcome the mythologies on which over-production and injustice have flourished.

In the 1300s we believed that lambs grew on trees. In the 1700s we allowed the cotton industry to enslave millions of people. In the 1990s (and still today) we turned a blind eye to a cotton industry that drained Uzbekistan's Aral Sea and trapped almost its entire population (from schoolchildren to professionals) in unethical labour during the cotton harvest.

From the start of the Industrial Revolution, cotton production has been fraught with pain, ignorance and exploitation. We tend to make the uninformed mistake of thinking about the fashion industry in a rhetorical way, as if the past holds all the answers for a better future, but this is far from being the case. Whether picked by slaves in the American South (where it became a staple of the

'*Colonialism is not a thing of the past, it is a modern economic reality; when we trace cotton, labour and silk routes they all map identically with colonial routes established a few hundred years ago. By empowering the existing system of exploitation of labour and resourcing, we are complying to the colonial model of extraction and destruction that ends up benefiting only a few on top of that pyramid scheme.*'

Céline Semaan, founder of the Slow Factory

local economy and was known as 'King Cotton') or diversifying to other countries after the American Civil War, cotton was mostly woven in UK sweatshops that were rife with child labour, before being exported globally and then sold via the East India Company, which was the precursor of imperialism and colonization.

In some ways, cotton paved the way for the democratization of fashion; it also exemplifies how fashion – frivolous at first glance – shapes history and dictates global politics.

In the late 18th century Marie Antoinette moved from her Austrian homeland to the palace of Versailles, upon marrying King Louis XVI. Unaccustomed to the eccentricities of pre-French Revolution attire, she would wear more casual clothes when left to her own devices. Instead of the luxurious silk robes worn by her circle of aristocratic friends, Marie Antoinette preferred simple cotton dresses for her off-duty wardrobe. In 1773 the painter Elisabeth Vigée-Lebrun depicted her in a cotton-gauze gown of this sort, resulting in one of the more dramatic and consequential paintings in history. Public reaction paralleled what you might expect to happen if the next First Lady of the United States had her official portrait painted in a tracksuit and trainers.

Of course, what erupts in scandal usually finds its way to popularity, and the *Chemise à la Reine* ultimately sparked an insatiable demand for cotton. At a time when many expected the American South to follow the suit of the North and end slavery, increased demands for cotton fibre spurred on the exploitation of cotton-pickers for decades to follow.

COTTON CONSEQUENCES

The large majority of today's cotton production is completely unsustainable, as conventional cotton-growing uses more water and toxic chemicals than any other crop.

☞ **Water usage:** According to figures from the Soil Association, growing cotton accounts for 69 per cent of the water footprint of textile fibre production; one kilogram of cotton takes as much as 10,000–20,000 litres of water. Our insatiable demand for King Cotton has almost completely dried out the Aral Sea, its water drained and diverted to provide for cotton irrigation and production, a fact that the UN describes as the greatest man-made environmental disaster of all time.

☞ **Soil contamination:** Cotton requires 200,000 tonnes of pesticides and 8 million tonnes of synthetic fertilizers to produce, every year. Like any mass-produced crop, pesticide use and monoculture farming lead to contaminated and nutrient-deficient soil. According to the Soil Exchange, organic cotton emits 46 per cent fewer carbon emissions than its conventional counterpart, in part because healthier soil acts as a carbon sink.

☞ **Food-chain contamination:** Cotton pesticides can also enter our food chain through certain processed foods, as well as meat and dairy products, since cows are often fed meals made from cottonseed.

- ☞ **Harm to wildlife:** Annually 24 per cent of all insecticides and 11 per cent of all pesticides in the world are used for growing cotton, yet it is estimated that less than 10 per cent of the chemicals applied to cotton fields are actually doing their job. The rest goes into the air, soil and water around the fields, harming or killing wildlife and severely affecting the ecology of the surrounding areas. The Pesticide Action Network estimates that nearly 1,000 people around the world die each year from pesticide poisoning, and an exponentially larger number suffer from related illnesses.

- ☞ **Harm to workers:** Cotton farming continues to be one of the biggest drivers of forced labour, including forced labour and child labour, across the fashion value chain (we'll discuss forced labour in more detail in Chapter 9). Beyond the worst forms of exploitation, cotton farming supports an estimated 250 million livelihoods around the world, according to Khursheed Ahmad Wani et al. in their *Handbook of Research on the Adverse Effects of Pesticide Pollution in Aquatic Ecosystems*, 2019. Given its huge impact on farmers and their families in developing nations, the global demand for ever-cheaper prices can profoundly harm these workers and their families.

GENETICALLY MODIFIED COTTON

The rules are simple, yet cruel: a traditional (non-genetically modified) plant is started from seeds. If a farmer buys a bag of seeds, he can grow his first plants and then harvest their seeds, beginning this cycle all over again without having to buy more new seeds. This lifecycle has been sustaining life on Earth for millennia.

Genetically Modified Organisms (GMOs) are different. When a farmer buys a bag of GMO seeds from the agriculture company Monsanto, Monsanto owns the patent to the future seeds that these plants create. Farmers are required to purchase new seeds each year and discard the seed from their previous year's harvest. This forced disruption in nature is monitored by so-called 'seed police' who search for and prosecute the seed reusers.

In a 2008 email to *Vanity Fair*, Monsanto's Darren Wallis said,

'Monsanto spends more than $2 million a day in research to identify, test, develop and bring to market innovative new seeds and technologies that benefit farmers. One tool in protecting this investment is patenting our discoveries and, if necessary, legally defending those patents against those who might choose to infringe upon them.'

In the global cotton-supply chain this 'tool' unfolds in the debts of poor, often illiterate farming communities, for the protection of one of the world's wealthiest companies. In India, where much of the world's cotton is grown, farmers become embroiled in a vicious circle of debt in order to buy GM seeds.

It is estimated that 95 per cent of all cotton grown in India is GM, and the misery it sows with its seeds includes regular spates of suicides (one farmer committed suicide every 30 minutes in India in 2009 alone).

ORGANIC COTTON

Switching to organic, non-GM cotton is widely seen as the only viable alternative to conventional cotton-growing, as organic cotton is grown without using toxic chemicals or GMOs, replenishing and maintaining soil fertility, reducing the use of toxic and persistent pesticides and fertilizers and encouraging a biologically diverse agriculture.

In addition, organic-cotton farmers use natural composting methods that promote healthier soil, and healthy soil acts like a sponge, soaking up water during floods and holding on to it for longer during droughts. Organic cotton is also watered differently, mostly relying on rain instead of having to extract water from the ground, which can put pressure on water supplies in local communities.

*'Cotton is a carbon sink and pulls CO_2 out of the
atmosphere and keeps it in the ground. Organic cotton
farming incorporates extra organic material into the
ground and keeps even more carbon in the ground,
thereby helping to cool the planet.'*

Katharine Hamnett, designer

Designer Katharine Hamnett has been advocating its use, to
the detriment of her own career, since the 1980s, is a true pioneer
in this field and the first to introduce organic cotton into mainstream fashion, starting in the '80s with her successful eponymous
label. Katharine is one of my personal heroes, a campaigning col-
league for more than 15 years and now also a close friend – I have
witnessed her commitment at first hand, and I value her work in
combining fashion design and advocacy above anyone else's. In
a recent conversation I had with her, she revealed some shocking
truths about the realities of GM and non-organic farming and the
potential benefits of switching to growing organic cotton instead.

In a nutshell: by switching to farming organically, farmers
would see a 50 per cent increase in profits, due to the reduction
in costs of chemical pesticides and fertilizers, combined with the
added income from the cash crops and food crops they would also
have to grow to rotate with their cotton, so as to be able to grow
it organically. This would enable them to better house, feed and
clothe their families, educate their children and afford healthcare,
which is not the case when they are growing conventional cotton.

Numerous deaths could be avoided by switching to organic
farming; every year there are thousands of accidental pesticide
poisonings and farmer suicides, due to pesticide debt.

Converting to organic farming would cut migration by making
cotton farming more viable. This would prevent farmers abandon-
ing their farms in order to head to the cities in search of alternative
work, in many cases dying along the way.

Organic cotton farming has immeasurable benefits, not only to the 100 million cotton farmers and their families, but also for biodiversity, soil fertility, fresh- and sea-water quality and for cutting greenhouse-gas emissions, which contribute to global warming:

- ☞ Organic cotton uses 91 per cent less water than conventional cotton.

- ☞ Chemical pesticides and herbicides used in non-organic farming contaminate our water supplies – groundwater, rivers and seas. These are chemicals derived from Second World War nerve gas, which are designed to kill and keep on killing – toxic to all life. Organic farming stops this grotesque environmental poisoning.

- ☞ While non-organic farming has been responsible for mass deforestation, wiping out all biodiversity from bees to birds, to worms and fungi, and causing desertification due to the micro-biological death of the soil, organic farming actually works with biodiversity, employing integrated pest management – an organic farming technique that makes use of natural pest predators instead of chemical pesticides.

- ☞ Converting to organic farming would drastically cut the nitrous-oxide (N_2O) emissions that come from chemical fertilizers. N_2O is a greenhouse gas 300 times heavier than carbon dioxide, and is known to be a major contributor to global warming and climate change.

BUYING BETTER: COTTON

- ☞ **Buy sustainable or organic cotton**: If we all looked for sustainable, non-genetically modified and/or organic cotton, and demanded the same from our retailers, we would be having an immensely positive impact on both people and the planet.
- ☞ **Research your retailer**: Many retailers pledged to switch to sustainable, non-GM or organic cotton by 2020, but if we, their customers, don't scrutinize them and hold them accountable on this promise, they most probably will not live up to their pledges. Acting on this is simple: vote with your wallet.
- ☞ **Demand better**: Whenever you are shopping, and wherever you do your regular shop (for T-shirts, socks, pants, shirts, bed linen, kitchen towels), look at the label and ask for a more sustainable alternative.
- ☞ **Buy to last**: This quote by fashion reporter Marc Bain sums it up for me: 'A landfill full of organic cotton T-shirts is still an overflowing landfill.' *How much* we consume is as important as *what* we consume. No point buying organic ingredients if you're going to chuck half your dish in the bin: you're still contributing to food waste. So there is no point buying anything, unless you seriously plan to keep it.

CARING FOR COTTON

Cotton washes easily and can withstand any temperature, making it an ideal fabric to care for. It is durable and strong, and shrink-resistant. Literally, check the label for washing instructions and that's it – no surprises there.

POLYESTER

Polyester textiles have existed for less than a century, yet they now comprise more than 50 per cent of our wardrobes and are the fastest-growing segment of textile production. It wasn't until 2002, after years of synthetic textiles exploding onto the high street, that King Cotton lost its place as the number-one textile in use.

When we look at all the ways that cotton has colonized and controlled the world, it should alarm us that polyester, a fibre that was invented less than a century ago, has so quickly surpassed such an ancient one. From an economic perspective, cotton's demise is a lesson in capitalism: a resource is only as good as its ability to remain the cheapest option.

When it comes to the invisible environmental damage from our clothes, polyester merits special attention, because almost everything we wear today contains it, and its effect on our environment is 100 per cent negative from extraction to aftercare. Put simply, and alarmingly, polyester is pure plastic, made from 100 per cent crude oil.

We are all aware of the visible impact of plastic pollution, particularly when it comes to our oceans and marine life – the Great Pacific Garbage Patch leaving no illusions about our intrusive plastic footprint – but recent research has highlighted an even scarier side-effect of our plastic addiction, and that is 'microplastics': invisible, splinter-like, deadly little buggers that are released from most synthetic fibres, but from polyester in particular, with up to 700,000 being released during each wash.

Staggeringly, the textile industry is responsible for nearly 35 per cent of all microplastic pollution. We have zero idea what effects they have, when ingested, breathed in and absorbed, but we do know that plastic pollution affects several bodily organs, and in particular endocrine functions in humans, and so it goes without saying that, once we undertake further studies on the side-effects of microplastics, we are unlikely to find them nourishing or beneficial.

CLOSING THE LOOP

Undoubtedly recycled polyester is better than virgin polyester, and we can rest assured that it will at least significantly reduce the environmental burden of extracting new oil from the ground, but unfortunately – in terms of wearing and washing it – it makes no difference whatsoever, as recycled polyester will shed micro-fibres as much as its virgin counterpart. Just because it says 'recycled' doesn't mean it is actually sustainable (more on this in Chapter 7, where we will look at recyclability options).

PET or polyethylene terephthalate, which is the chemical compound in polyester, is also the type of plastic used in plastic bottles and other types of packaging. In 1993 the clothing company Patagonia became the first manufacturer to use recycled plastic polyester in its products. This craze for recycled PET was hailed as a real solution to deal with a real problem, until it became clear that the huge demand for this seemingly miracle-fabric actually distorted the way we were procuring the raw materials with which it was made. In short, there weren't enough recoverable plastic bottles in circulation (or, quite simply, it became burdensome to create the systems to effectively recuperate them). Stories started to surface of unscrupulous companies actually producing new plastic bottles that were never intended to be filled with water or fizzy drinks, only to be turned straight into fibre.

This is still, apparently, happening to this very day, and it is almost impossible to discern which fleece materials are genuinely made from waste and which are made from fraud. This circular system – that of empty bottles = yarn = fleece – is a sophisticated loop of recovery, transport and remanufacturing, long and slow. But why not make new plastic bottles from old plastic bottles? If we'd spent the last 25 years enforcing laws ensuring that all new plastic bottles had to be made from 100 per cent recycled plastic – thereby encouraging recycling in a proper closed loop, rather than diverting materials to become a part of another cycle – it would have been more efficient and logical, because, although in principle a 100 per cent recycled PET fabric is in turn completely recyclable, the other materials that are added to an item of clothing, such as borders, zips and buttons, are not, and we do not have in place a proven, effective system for recycling our synthetic clothing. So going from bottle (discarded or not) to clothing simply diverts from a virtuous loop into an unnecessarily long-winded, unregulated and highly cheatable system.

CARING FOR POLYESTER

Wash polyester garments as little as you can. This in turn means do not buy polyester garments or clothes made from fabrics that contain a high percentage of polyester, if they are going to need frequent washing – school-uniform shirts, for example, which your children wear next to their skin five days a week and are washed at least twice a week. Go the extra mile and, if you can, spend the extra penny to source 100 per cent cotton over poly.

Polyester is a durable, low-maintenance fibre that should be kept for ever, because, as it is made from plastic, it will take more than 800 years to biodegrade – and this is one of the biggest problems we are facing right now, because fast, disposable fashion is almost exclusively made from polyester. Polyester is a material that we should be using to make coats and outerwear, and garments that can be spot-cleaned and sponged; evening wear would be a great option – take a gorgeous, 1960s vintage piece, for example, worn once at a party, which can be refreshed with a quick shower steam the next day (or the day after that, depending on the hangover) and kept in your wardrobe until its next outing without fear of being moth-eaten in the meantime.

In her brilliant publication *Shirt Stories*, Professor Rebecca Earley, one of the world's experts on recycling and upcycling in the fashion industry, enlists the help of many of her colleagues to explain the role of polyester in our everyday clothes. Holly McQuillan (senior lecturer in design and author) explains it clearly:

'We make value judgements on polyester, primarily that it's cheap and therefore only useful for garments that are cheap. However, by treating it this way we place it into the very context where it will cause the most damage. Perhaps, since polyester is literally here to stay, we need to use only what we already have, and value it more – it's what we do with it that counts.'

Becky Earley's take on it is equally important, and she sent me this quote to further contextualize how we can begin to reason positively, as consumers and as an industry, when it comes to the use of this material:

'It is crucial that we understand how to transition from our reliance on fossil fuel-based materials without causing mass-scale structural violence. To drive industry change we need material roadmaps which have been drawn up by recognizing both the benefits and pitfalls that come with materials like polyester. We will only get businesses to change if we show them the way forward – how to transition – and this future scenario needs much more research, which needs to happen very quickly now.'

Rebecca Earley, *Shirt Stories*, 2019

PROBLEMATIC POLY

Sometimes it is impossible to find a quick fix, a 'one size fits all' solution, especially when it comes to kids' clothing and school uniforms in particular, or certain frequently worn and frequently washed items, such as activewear and underwear. In some cases the only solution is to switch to sustainable, non-GM and organic cotton, but this isn't always available or affordable.

When it comes to school uniforms, we know that one chemical in particular, perfluorooctanoic acid (which is used to make outdoor clothing more resistant to stains), has been found to be carcinogenic in animal trials. We also know that many children are allergic to synthetic materials; there are alternatives in circulation, but dare I say it, not nearly enough.

For activewear, the use of heavily polluting and highly toxic materials makes no sense whatsoever. Just picture it: millions of health freaks worldwide, exercising, doing yoga, jogging, meditating, channelling their personal well-being as a priority in today's stressful life . . . all the while unknowingly absorbing plastic toxicants and other contaminants with each drop of sweat, and then washing it all out into the public waterways in their daily wash. It's enough to make you choke on your kale and spirulina juice!

The health and well-being industry is constantly evolving in the exercises, superfoods and wellness products that represent today's ideal of the pinnacle of health. So surely it's time for the toxicity of bum-hugging exercise tights to be exposed. The bottom line is this: always look for natural fibres, or non-toxic sustainable alternatives instead. An old cotton T-shirt will serve you just as well as a moisture-wicking performance tank, and will probably cost you a fraction of the price.

NYLON

Like polyester, nylon (scientifically known as polyamide) is a plastic-based material that sheds microplastics and that stems from crude oil. While current research suggests that nylon sheds significantly fewer fibres than similar polyester garments, its plastic origins still mean that it must be washed carefully.

Nylon, for the most part, is found in activewear and tights. Its versatility sees it used in most bathing suits, blended with elastane; and its ability to be tightly woven makes it a popular choice for windproof wear.

Of course, it isn't only employed in clothes, as nylon also makes up camping tents, fishing nets and those now-iconic Longchamp bags. Given its wide array of uses, nylon is a good candidate for recycling innovations. One of these of note is ECONYL, which uses fishing nets and other found ocean plastic to create a recycled nylon that can forever remain in the loop. While other recycling innovations might see found materials made into a swimsuit, which is then discarded and returns to landfill, ECONYL can continually be regenerated into new yarn.

Nylon tights are my biggest problem. I'm sure a lot of us are guilty of throwing away many a pair after the first ladder appears (more often than not in household bins, as opposed to being adequately disposed of in textile banks). Yet these disposably designed bits of nylon can take up to 40 years to biodegrade.

I love tights. For me, a good pair of tights makes an outfit, almost more than the shoes. I tend to buy good-quality tights for durability, and I have many pairs, so that I can rotate them; but tights break – that's just a fact of life. My keeping system works this way: once a pair of tights starts to ladder, I will prevent it going any further by blocking said laddering with transparent nail varnish; or, if I'm out and don't have any, I will use bar soap instead, albeit temporarily. My broken tights live to the left-hand side of the tights drawer, and I continue to use them regardless, underneath trousers or long skirts for warmth, sometimes for years. Eventually I cut them up: I save the feet by cutting at mid-calf, then let them roll and use them as popsocks; and I slice the rest of the leg into 10 cm-wide strips, which I use as hairbands.

I am no longer a fan of woollen tights, but when I was, I would eventually turn them into tops, by cutting out the gusset and cutting off the feet, crocheting around the raw edges to stop them from fraying, then turning them upside down to wear as a crop top.

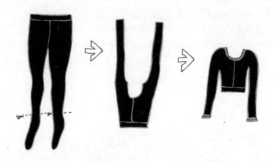

ACRYLIC

Like its plastic partners, acrylic is an oil-based offender in the textile world. Its kinked structure is designed to cheaply mimic the properties of wool, which is why it's found on the composition labels of many cardigans and jumpers. Acrylic isn't such a great standalone fibre, because its high susceptibility to pilling means that most synthetic sweaters see acrylic blended with some degree of wool or other synthetic yarn.

LINEN

Linen is one of the oldest textile fibres, its earliest remains having been found in Switzerland, Georgia and Egypt, dating back to prehistoric times.

Today it is commonly known as a sustainable fibre, because its cultivation requires little pesticide use and minimal water, and it can grow even in poor soil. Yet unfortunately linen represents only a small percentage of the global fibre market share, perhaps because its labour-intensive manufacturing process makes it more expensive than other alternatives. Linen also gains its sustainable credentials because the 'waste' from the above processes can be used to make linseed oil, a purposeful by-product that makes the entire flax plant useful.

CARING FOR LINEN

Linen is less easy to care for than cotton, as it can shrink. Its porous nature also makes it less ideal for spot-cleaning, and I find that occasionally when I do, the stain gets worse, as it expands and sinks into the fabric. Linen also creases easily (and no amount of ironing will get rid of the more stubborn creases), so you have to like the crumpled look to appreciate this material. As far as its multiple properties go, I find linen incredibly luxurious as a seasonal fabric and only wear it in the summer, when it can feel cool on the skin despite the sweltering heat. And nothing – NOTHING – beats linen bed sheets.

HEMP

Hemp is a weed that grows spontaneously worldwide and requires very little maintenance. Its properties and varied usage are the stuff of legend, and humans have used it for millennia to make everything from fibres to oils.

Hemp is a miracle crop that originated in China and the Middle East, but rapidly flourished wherever it was introduced. Easy to grow, versatile and adaptable, it was used to make paper and building materials as well as a wide spectrum of fabrics, from durable industrial textiles to fashion items.

It is hard to imagine now how predominant it was, considering that the production of hemp has been completely eradicated in favour of cotton crops and the increased demand for synthetic materials, but up to the Second World War hemp reigned unchallenged: a convenient, efficient crop that required less water, as well as acting as a powerful aerator for the soil in which it grew.

Eventually hemp was publicly demonized, ostensibly because of the marijuana connection (marijuana is indeed a strain of hemp, notorious for its mood-altering side-effects), but in truth so that rich individuals and corporations with interests in paper and pesticides could monopolize the system. A rich culture and an incredibly sustainable plant was rendered near-obsolete – a huge loss to people, nature and industry.

Today hemp has a bad name as the 'ugly' face of eco-fashion. But it shouldn't do. Instead it deserves the attention and the innovation to bring it fully into fashion.

MAN-MADE CELLULOSIC FIBRES *(MMCFs)*

Like the natural fabrics described above (cotton, linen and hemp), man-made cellulosic fibres are made from plants. The difference between these and true 'natural' fibres is that MMCFs require a considerable amount of chemical processing to turn rigid plant matter, like trees and stems, into soft clothing material.

But don't be confused by the name. It's important to remember that all materials – 'natural', 'man-made' or 'synthetic' – are derived from natural resources, be it plant, animal or fossil fuels. And just as all materials begin as nature, so all materials are indeed 'man-made'.

Dilys Williams, an academic and head of the Centre for Sustainable Fashion, put it best when she told BBC Radio 4 in August 2019, 'The two fundamental parts of anything that is next to your skin right now is nature and labour.'

ARTIFICIAL SILK

Before rayon (which is how most MMCFs are referred to), all fashion fabrics were essentially natural. Humans were basically wearing cotton, linen, silk, wool and animal skins without much variation. Rayon, which was first marketed under the slogan 'artificial silk', is made from plant matter, but the chemical processes needed to turn this matter into slinky fabric are so strenuous that we can't really say rayon is a natural material – hence, 'man-made-cellulose'.

Most rayon is made from wood pulp, and most wood pulp is transformed into rayon through a process once known as the 'viscose method'. Rayon is the umbrella name for a series of cellulose-based materials, the most common of which is viscose.

For the vast majority of viscose, which is made from trees, there are two main environmental sins that we will focus on in this book. The first is that the volume and intensity of the chemicals required to turn wood into fabric are completely toxic.

Changing Markets, an organization working to clean up the viscose supply chain, has found that the carbon disulphide (CS_2) used in making viscose is an endocrine-disruptor (causer of infertility) and has been linked with mental illness among viscose factory workers. In their 2019 survey of 90 global fashion brands, Changing Markets found that more than 25 per cent of them had absolutely no responsible viscose policies in place.

In the 1970s Lyocell, a variation of rayon, was developed. While more costly to manufacture than viscose, it is able to transform plant matter into fabric with minimal chemical intervention. The patent was eventually bought by the Lenzing company and today we mostly know it by its trade name, Tencel.

BEST PRACTICE AND SCALE

In the nearly 200 years since rayon's inception, there have been many variations of it that have been dressed in all kinds of fashion marketing. While innovations like Tencel help to lower the chemical consequences of the materials, the simple fact that many of us are commonly wearing trees should cause us to reflect on fashion's profound drain on precious natural resources.

Even before viscose reaches the harsh chemical phase in production, it pillages a critical ecosystem: forests. Textile Exchange reports that global production of man-made cellulose textiles has doubled since the 1990s. And according to the forest stewardship organization Canopy, around 150 million trees are deforested every year to be turned into textiles. With fashion production – and viscose – on the rise, it is urgent that we protect ancient forests, and harvest wood responsibly and restoratively.

CARING FOR RAYON

Viscose shrinks, and shrinks, and shrinks, even at a very low heat. This will vary hugely from garment to garment, and quality is an important indicator, as cheap viscose is remarkably worse than more expensive varieties. I don't own much viscose for this reason, because I am not confident about washing it, so I tend to sponge or steam – but in all honesty, I have seen even such mild interventions result in localized shrinkage (particularly on jersey viscose).

WOOL

If I could choose a fabric – any fabric – for my desert-island disc, it would be wool. To my mind, nothing beats it. Wool works with everything and for every occasion: it's warm and cosy, fluffy or rough, knitted or woven. I wear it directly on the skin; I sleep under a wool duvet; and I find certain types of wool, such as *'fresco lana'* and wool crêpe, infinitely more elegant than any silk for evening wear. Since my designer days are over, I have donated all my best leftover fabrics to young designers in the UK, my last remaining rolls having gone to Phoebe English to rework them for her 2020 womenswear collection. I managed to home all my remnants, except for a roll of black wool crêpe, which I refuse to part with.

The use of wool may not be as ancient as that of linen, flax and hemp, but it nevertheless dates back more than 5,000 years, when ancient humans spun and wove the hairs of sheep in Mesopotamia, the Middle East and parts of Europe. Around 1900 BC British weaving emerged, and English wools became a widely traded commodity throughout the Roman Empire.

Wool also gave rise to a whole new textile industry and a rich culture to accompany it. In 1300 the town of Prato in Tuscany developed a wool guild, or *Arte della Lana*. Later, in the 1500s, Spanish wool industries emerged (merino wool originates in Spain). As British and Spanish colonies were established around the world, they brought sheep with them all the way to the Americas and Australia.

Interestingly, when looking at present-day deforestation practices in the Amazon and other places, it seems as though the clearing of land is a modern phenomenon, but wool represents an early iteration of this practice: in the mid-18th century the Scottish 'Highland Clearances' saw tenants forcibly removed by landowners, to be replaced by large-scale sheep farms. Many of them were forced to migrate as a result, so the great-great-grandchildren of Scottish immigrants in North America, the Australian Labor Party and the establishment of towns and trading ports across the world all share a catalyst: wool.

WOOL CONSEQUENCES

Mulesing: The most ethically questionable practice in modern sheep husbandry is what's known as mulesing. Consider this the livestock version of pesticides. Wool flocks are at risk of flystrike, a rather graphic condition where flies lay their eggs in the skin folds of sheep, and the maggots, once hatched, bury themselves in the sheep's wool and feed off their skin. Yet it's the preventative method that causes the greatest offence in the world of animal welfare: mulesing, in order to prevent flystrike, is the process of surgically removing strips of skin from the buttocks of the sheep, decreasing the likelihood of soiled areas that would attract flies.

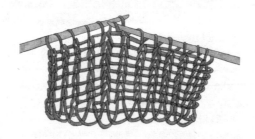

Impact on the land: The land inhabited by sheep is non-arable, meaning that other crops can't be grown on the same land, because sheep are grazing creatures and tend to eat the grasses to the point where the land is no longer 'living'.

Biodegradable?: As for all wool being ecologically biodegradable, it is, in its purest form: hairs. However, once treated, spoiled with toxic chemicals and intensive processes (as well as the usual culprit – quantity), it ceases to degrade naturally and presents its own problems in landfill, from the release of methane gas into the atmosphere to contamination of the soil.

Of course, not all wool is created equally. Look for the Responsible Wool Standard, an independent certification that addresses both the ethical and environmental concerns around wool production. Put simply, the RWS ensures that flocks are raised in accordance with the five animal freedoms (including no mulesing) and ensures responsible land management.

CARING FOR WOOL

In my opinion, wool is best washed at zero heat (or lower than 20 degrees), just in case, because it does shrink with heat. Washed with care, wool is a remarkably long-lasting fibre, although it does tend to lose its shape after multiple washes, which is why it is always best to avoid a fast spin at the end of the wash and to dry it flat on a towel, rather than hung on a washing line. Do not tumble dry it, or hang it on a hot radiator.

WOOL DECOY

☞ One of my favourite tips to avoid moths was passed to me by Mr Barni in Prato. Barni was the owner of an enormous second-hand clothing warehouse, from which I bought tonnes and tonnes of clothes when I had my upcycling brand. This tip is so simple, yet so efficacious, that it almost beggars belief. Basically it starts from the premise that moths have taste and preferences, and will be happier nestling in your camel or Shetland more than in merino or mohair. So if you include a 'decoy' in your wardrobe and/or drawers, they will flock to that and leave the rest reasonably in peace. For moth preference, the softer the protein fibres, the better, so find the scraps of an old sweater (Shetland wool works well for me every time) or a ball of yarn.

☞ Some of the people I have tried to pass this tip on to find it quite repellent, but I see no difference between a wool decoy and those horrendous, chemically impregnated sticky tapes that moths get stuck to. ✺

HOW TO MEND WOOL

My mother unravels and then reknits. She has been doing this for ever, as far as I can remember: she'll buy something second-hand, or look in her own wardrobe, and create something new. Unravelling knits is a completely brilliant way to repurpose old knitwear – probably the most effective, if you know how to knit. It won't matter if a piece is broken, with holes or stains, because you can interrupt the thread to get rid of the unwanted bit, tie a tiny knot and get unravelling/knitting again. The only trick is that in order to unravel successfully, the piece in question needs to be fully fashioned, not cut and sewn.

OTHER HAIRS

CASHMERE

The Kashmir goat produces hair three times warmer than wool, with a softer, silkier touch, and is widely considered the pinnacle of luxury. Once upon a time the animal was specific to the Kashmir region, but its profitability brought flocks beyond Mongolia and Tibet to China, Iran, India and Afghanistan. Often the goats are sheared midwinter, when their fleece is the warmest, which can leave them freezing (sometimes fatally) in the cold climates where they live.

Furthermore, the overbreeding of Kashmir goats is destroying the landscapes in their native home: too many grazing animals are turning the lush grasslands into deserts, particularly in Mongolia.

MOHAIR

This is a fluffy, lightweight fibre from Angora goats. These goats are native to Turkey, but have been domesticated across Africa. Like Kashmir goats, Angora goats have less fat than sheep, making them susceptible to pneumonia and to freezing, once they've been shorn. Mohair wool is lightest and shiniest when the goat is relatively young, which makes the fibre more expensive, as it can't be obtained throughout the animal's entire life.

ANGORA

This is where it gets confusing, because while the Angora *goat* makes mohair wool, the Angora *rabbit* makes angora wool. In Turkey, England, France and other countries, Angora rabbits have long been raised for their luxurious hairs, which need to be shorn every few months. Yet as the fashion industry has pivoted towards mass production, the angora industry has left for China, where live plucking (among other animal-welfare concerns) has made the possibility of ethical angora into an oxymoron.

SILK

I never leave the house without a large, square silk scarf. I have a huge collection: my most precious are proper Hermès ones (inherited mostly from my mother and grandmother), but I have been picking them up in charity and vintage stores, greedily, for years. They are incredibly useful and, when it comes to multi-functionality, one scarf can be several other things: a belt, a hair accessory (looks amazing tied around a messy bun), a top, an improvised pillow case if wrapped around a soft jumper or puffer coat when travelling, or, if I am accidentally without a sponge, I will wet its corner and use it to remove stains.

I have even used silk scarves as evening handbags (really cute, tied in a big knot, so that they look like a little sack) and spread them on the floor for picnics at the park. I used to wrap them around my daughters when they were small, as an improvised sarong after a day at the beach (or just to let them wear it as dressing-up on the go).

> 1. Take a large silk foulard (cotton will do too, like a large bandana – at least 80 cm square) and fold it in half to make a rectangle.
>
> 2. Sew a length of ribbon or decorative trimming approx. 40 cm long to both corners on one side of the rectangle, and sew the other end of the ribbon to the corners on the other side.
>
> 3. Wear your new top with your arms through the holes and the ribbon at the back.

Once you get the hang of it, that ribbon can be almost anything: back in the day when this top was one of our brand's best sellers (as featured in the *Telegraph* magazine in 2003). I often used lingerie elastic on which I sewed mother-of-pearl buttons. In a rush for a party with nothing to wear, and nothing to sew with, I once made one with safety pins and shoe laces!

WORN WORMS

Like wool, silk is a fabric of animal protein. It is generated from the filaments of insects, which they extrude to form cocoons. Technically speaking, silk can be made from any bug that envelops itself in a cocoon or spins itself a web. Spider silk, in fact, has long been portrayed as a miracle-fibre – strong enough to stop bullets, yet fine enough to weave the lightest of materials. Of course, spider silk has never fully been harnessed in textile production on any reproducible scale. Its properties and characteristics have spurred science experiments and been the subject of a major case-study in the field of biomimicry – a design practice that seeks to imitate nature's most impressive feats. From genetic engineering to synthetic biology, spider silk remains a Holy Grail for the future of textile innovation.

But what about real silk? The naturally iridescent material drove trade between Europe and Asia for centuries, and today – despite being synonymous with luxury – silk comprises only 0.1 per cent of the total global fibre production for textiles. This silk doesn't come from a spider, but from a domesticated silkworm during its cocooned transition to moth.

Silk has its roots in China, where early people (around 2500 BC) discovered that the yarn of a single worm's cocoon could be unravelled and outstretched to reach a kilometre in length. The triangular cross-section of the filament creates a shiny surface when it is spun and woven.

The process of farming silkworms, collecting their cocoons and boiling them alive spread from China to India, and then throughout Asia, the Middle East and into Europe until the 19th century. The laborious process of farming the animals and repopulating them was a vast contributor to the rise of synthetic materials. The very existence of rayon/viscose (see page 103), the 'first synthetic material', rests on scientists' endeavours to create a material with the properties of silk at the cost of cotton.

From an animal-rights perspective, silk's pain-points lie in the harvesting of live cocoons in order to make the material. Cocoons must be collected before the worm-turned-moth exits its home, otherwise the 1,000-metre filament will be broken by the exiting creature. In this way the creation of the fabric kills the animals that eject the yarn, making it wholly unvegetarian.

'Peace silk' (also called Ahimsa silk) has been developed as a reaction to the problem, by collecting cocoons *after* the moths exit, and creating a more broken fibre where the shorter filaments must be spun in order to form a continuous yarn.

Another forward-thinking approach to this material is the new introduction of organic certification. While it's not vegetarian, organic silk farming can contribute positively to crop diversity. One such example is in Thailand, where cassava plants are grown with their roots being eaten by local communities, their leaves fed to the silkworm cultures and the worm faeces returned to cultivate the cassava as fertilizer.

CARING FOR SILK

I find silk remarkably easy to care for, provided you know its properties and take a close look at it before you wash it. Silks can vary hugely in quality – from slippery satins to more textured natural weaves – but all require a delicate wash, preferably at a heat lower than 30 degrees. For best results, iron when damp, but ensure that you place a towel between the iron and the fabric.

Fibreshed: from farm to wardrobe

Just as we are beginning to understand the effect that the fashion industry has on water, so we need to understand the profound relationship between fashion and soil, because almost every material we wear originates and affects our soil in one way or another, whether we are extracting resources from it, or planting cotton, or farming animals, or cutting down trees to make cellulosic fibres.

The relationship between fashion and agriculture isn't something that springs immediately to mind when we think about our clothes, yet agriculture – and the use of soil for growing fabrics, or for farming and feeding those animals that are used for fashion – is as important as water, and the negative impact of industry has affected them both immensely.

Decades of intensive farming, and the increased use of pesticides and fertilizers full of toxicants, have impaired our soil's capacity to absorb water, making it dryer, arid and less fertile.

For this reason we are often in the grip of a very unnatural imbalance: we can be both in a state of drought and simultaneously suffer flooding. The arid soil, deprived of trees, roots and a holistic, natural crop rotation, is incapable of absorption, and nutrients and water rush through it, not sinking into it – a bit like water does off a duck's back, as they say.

Recently activism has gone back to the ground, literally, and more and more attention is being paid to the role of soil for a sustainable future, with a return to biodynamic farming and other very traditional systems for agriculture now being explored globally. In fashion this works by planting and harvesting organic fibres such as cotton, linen and hemp. This counter-movement is called Fibreshed and counts numerous designers and celebrity endorsements, including that of model-turned-campaigner Arizona Muse.

LEATHER

Leather is a controversial and highly polluting material, one of the biggest offenders when it comes to human and environmental exploitation in terms of fashion. For years, fashion brands have justified its use as a 'by-product' of the meat industry, essentially shirking their responsibility over farming, deforestation, slaughtering and all the other negatives associated with livestock, by laying fault at the source: the food sector. But this isn't an accurate picture of either industry.

In Brazil, cattle farming has driven deforestation and spurred the catastrophic Amazon rainforest fires, which were famously at their worst in autumn 2019. Here, the hides industry is hardly a by-product, with leather accounting for a quarter of the export value of Brazilian cattle products between 2006 and 2010, according to Natalie F. Walker et al. in 'From Amazon Pasture to the High Street', 2013.

So as we dive into leather, let's first of all remove ourselves from the excuse that leather is a by-product. Like any other resource on this Earth, supply is driven by our demand. Without question, the processes around leather production are among the most damaging, both socially – as supply workers employed in the leather supply chain are exposed to excessive amounts of chemicals that can cause side-effects, such as skin reactions, digestive problems and kidney damage – and environmentally, because much debris that is the result of leather production is dumped in rivers, affecting public waterways, which are pumped full of chromium, lead, arsenic and other toxicants.

Tanning is the most toxic phase in leather processing. Today, 80–90 per cent of leather hides in the world are tanned using chromium, which is a solution of highly toxic chemicals, acids and salts (including chromium sulfate). In developing countries such as Bangladesh, where the leather and footwear industry is the second-largest generator of revenue, tanneries are largely unregulated danger zones, where abuses of human rights and environmental standards are the norm and not the exception.

One of the biggest issues in the leather supply chain takes place even before the animals themselves are reared into husbandry. It is the creation of the pasture itself that has profoundly shifted global ecosystems and depleted this Earth's most precious carbon sink: our rainforests. Before the industrialization of animal agriculture, ranchers and farmers settled on land fit for their crops or livestock, but as global demand for resources has turned farming into intensive factory work, we have had to change wild lands into pastures.

Nowhere has this had a more terrifying impact than in the Amazon rainforest. Home to roughly 10 per cent of species on the planet, the Amazon rainforest is expected to reach 27 per cent deforestation by 2030, according to WWF (https://wwf.panda.org/our_work/forests/deforestation_fronts2/deforestation_in_the_amazon/). While the Amazon and other rainforests in Madagascar and Indonesia burn, we must question our habits more urgently than ever – the meat industry, and the leather-goods industry who uses its by-products must take full responsibility for the environmental degradation they have inflicted on the planet and must push towards a radical rebalancing to decrease their combined footprints.

EXOTIC EXPLOITATION

The 'leather as a by-product' argument further disintegrates when we consider the use of exotic leathers, as we certainly aren't mass-consuming lizards and crocodiles, or pythons. For years, PETA (People for the Ethical Treatment of Animals) has been documenting the mistreatment of alligators, crocodiles and other reptiles that luxury-goods brands have deemed perfectly acceptable up until the day before yesterday – and we're talking about the at-scale systemic torture of beautiful creatures to make shoes, bags and bloody belts.

Although a concerted effort is being made by brands to redeem themselves after decades of animal cruelty, this move is super-recent and feels desperate and disingenuous. What took them so long to understand that selling millions of shoes, bags, belts, wallets and phone cases meant cruelly slaughtering millions of animals for their skins?

PETROCHEMICAL ALTERNATIVES

Moving on to the next hurdle: vegan leather, aka fake leather or PVC, which is, of course, plastic. It's cheap, and is used to make vast amounts of accessories that are discarded just as fast as clothes are. Admittedly, the negative impact that the production of real leather has on the planet is increasingly seen as much higher than that of non-leather, and huge steps have been made in PVC innovation; there are now much better options in use. Nevertheless, the majority of PVC on the market is still of the lower-quality, more invasive kind, and it is being used excessively and unscrupulously, considering its negative impact.

The statistic in MIT's 'Sustainable Apparel Materials' of 2015 that says we are producing 150 billion garments a year doesn't take into account accessories, and the reality is that we are probably acquiring and disposing of as many cheap accessories as we are cheap clothing – and, unfortunately, cheap accessories and shoes are more likely to be made with cheap plastic.

Take your average cheap bag: PVC, metals, plastic buttons, polyester appliqué, nylon lining, labels . . . bought and then discarded. Each cheap bag (and cheap shoe and cheap hairband) is awash with components that are as badly glued on as they are badly matched, made to be broken quickly, but not to break up in landfill.

One consideration to note here is the idea of the *Jevon's paradox*. This economic term is an important one in considering whether the sustainability efforts of a brand have any meaning or impact. It's defined as 'When technological progress . . . increases the efficiency with which a resource is used, but the rate of consumption of that resource rises'. This means that if a company harnesses technology or 'progress' to improve the footprint of a product, such as replacing virgin polyester with recycled polyester, it might cut the impact of that product by, say, 30 per cent. But if that company enjoys endless growth, consumption of this product may rise by, say, 50 per cent. Ultimately, the sustainability measures taken by the brand are outpaced by the brand's endless endeavour to grow its profits.

Vegan leather, aka plastic leather, aka fake leather may be better for the environment after all, but the question it begs is more akin to the 'Would you rather go on a date with a rapist or a murderer?' scenario, because in this case better is by no means good; and considering how bad the bad is, better is absolutely not good enough.

INNOVATION

The future of leather is colourful. And potentially edible too, if we look at the ingredients that are being proposed!

From dyeing leather with bark, berries and other natural colourants, to systems for processing it without the dreaded chromium, to entirely new raw materials such as fish skins, mushrooms, pineapple and other fruits, the race is on to break this vicious cycle and turn it virtuous.

FAKING IT

In a supply chain where there is no transparency, there is no knowing where laws are being broken; and when it comes to fake bags and imitations, we know pretty much the same as what we know about most of the real ones.

Luxury brands go to painstaking measures to bring our attention to the fact that imitations are made with lesser-quality materials and manufactured in exploitative conditions, and that the people who sell them are often vulnerable immigrants in the grip of criminal trafficking gangs; but when it comes to the Real Thing, brands give us little or no indication that authentic products carry better human-rights and environmental credibility.

If brands were to embrace transparency, and publish their supply chains so that we could really see the making of our goods, only then would it feel accurate to depict the counterfeit supply chain as a lesser production model.

To add to the confusion, sometimes fake bags are actually real, part of a factory over-production or discarded for being barely visibly damaged at source; and the real fakes, the imposters, are often produced in the very same factory complexes, by the same skilled workers who made the designer bags. If we take into account luxury designers' use of modern, non-leather materials such as PVC and nylon, and today's lower-quality luxury standards, it's easy to see that fakes – once the inferior, clumsy, apologetic imitation of the aspirational Real Thing – could in fact be twin products separated at birth, with only one of them anointed with a logo.

Having said that, we do know, or strongly suspect, that fake-goods revenues feed criminal gangs, that their value chain itinerary is connected with human trafficking, and that they are illegal, and so, even though we are flooded with fake items, we certainly shouldn't indulge; but when it comes to comparing the *product* and, in so many respects, provenance and make, many of today's fakes are as good as the real thing.

For me, nothing beats the adrenaline rush that comes from spotting a designer bag in mint condition in a charity shop, which – considering mass consumption and accelerated disposal – happens more and more frequently. Until the day that mainstream luxury-goods brands can provide me with an impeccable product pedigree of 100 per cent transparency and disclosure on the make, and the provenance of ALL its materials (from leather to metals and everything in between), and we go back to a model where quality, not cost, is the prerogative, I see no point in buying their offerings; I do not call it luxury, and it does not deserve its high price, or its reputation.

As an alternative, I prefer to invest in a more artisanal product: something handmade, constructed with healthier materials and saner principles.

THE RISE AND FALL

I was lucky enough to inherit two Gucci bags from my grand-mother, both made in the 1940s. I then went on to receive a more modern version as a wedding present from my in-laws; looking at them all in detail, it is as if the history of leatherwork and the luxury-goods brands' approach to quality was engraved in all three – a visible display of deterioration that still leaves me furious.

One of the older bags is an evening clutch, made entirely in silk satin, black on the outside and powder-pink inside. The satin is so lush, so thick, so smooth, it looks like double cream or melted chocolate. The outer beadwork is exceptionally fine and deli-cate, a little universe of tiny black glass beads, which have been hand-sewn so precisely, and so expertly, that they are still com-pletely intact after 80 years of regular use. It was given to me at some point in my thirties, and I wear it almost every time I go to a black-tie event or somewhere very fancy, which, as I work in fashion, is not an altogether rare occasion. Inside, as well as the luscious satin, it has two reinforced pockets, one at each side, in different shapes and sizes: one for visiting cards and the other a perfect fit for a powder case. The clutch mechanism is still crisp, intact, functioning perfectly, despite its years.

The second bag from my grandmother is leather, also a clutch, but now unfortunately in a sorrier state and no longer in use, simply because – being a daytime bag – it was worn more often.

My grandmother used it regularly, and I used it every single day for at least five or six years during the 1990s. Eventually it

OF A GUCCI HANDBAG

broke, but I forgave it for having a few tears at the side seam, and only stopped using it when my favourite lipstick was lost as a result.

My eulogy is for the way it was constructed, and in particular the inside of the bag (Gucci people, read on, please): it had three compartments, the middle one envelope-thin, and six different pockets, each of different shapes, each with a different function, PLUS a little leather pen-loop. There is a pocket for lipstick, one for face powder, it even has one smaller pocket inside a larger one. It is so generous, practical and thoughtfully designed.

The third bag is a classic modern Gucci from the late 1990s, but a train crash compared to its predecessors: the opening/closing mechanism felt wobbly and uncertain from the minute I received it, and the tiny, fiddly key to secure it (which is so impractical that I assumed it was but a useless decoration) genuinely had to be used regularly to prevent the lock from opening at the slightest touch. Inside it is heartbreakingly disappointing: no compartments, just one hollow void. Only one side pocket, the size of a credit card, but so thin it wouldn't fit more than one or two.

Have you also noticed how quality is going down the drain? It pains me that my kids will never know the difference between what is lush and what merely imitates lushness superficially. It bothers me that we are perpetually sold a lie: that we are told that something is exquisite when it is, at best, little over mediocre.

FHURRRRRR

For millennia, fur made life possible for people living in parts of the world where human skin wasn't enough protection from freezing temperatures and arctic conditions. From northern Canada to Siberian Russia, the pelts of seals, wolves and foxes have served as essential protection.

Interestingly, I once heard a story that it was the invention of the needle to sew animal hides that guaranteed our survival during one of the Northern Hemisphere Ice Ages. It sounds very plausible: before the invention of the needle, imagine all that running, and hunting, while wearing loosely fitting animal skins – very impractical – until suddenly things started taking shape (literally) and hides were sewn together. I imagine that sleeves might have made an appearance at that time. Clothing became snug and warm and allowed for movement – hence our survival. Furthermore, global fur trades have spurred on globalization throughout the world, first between Russia and Germany, and then opening up North America to European colonization.

The case against real fur, and the animal-welfare movement, has been raging for more than 30 years. The history of protest against wearing fur has been hard-fought, with countless buckets of fake blood flung, and naked people declaring their contempt over the years. PETA first launched its infamous 'I'd Rather Go Naked Than Wear Fur' campaign in 1991. The now instantly recognizable ads have featured dozens of celebrities stripping down over the years, with everyone from The Go-Go's to Pamela Anderson and Khloe Kardashian featuring in the iconic protest posters.

Until not that long ago, fur was a defining material for luxury fashion houses, with Stella McCartney being the renegade lone wolf with her pioneering vegetarian brand. In recent years, however, banning fur has become the expected position to be taken by premium brands and retailers: in 2017 Gucci announced it would remove all real fur from its collections, and a year later the city of Los Angeles banned the sale and manufacturing of furs, to take effect from 2020.

In September 2017 London Fashion Week attendees were met

with more than 250 protesters, donned in fake blood, blocking the entrances for a three-day demonstration. As reported in *The Guardian* on 16 February 2018, the protests were a response to a statement that the British Fashion Council released: 'the BFC does not intervene in the creative process . . . does not dictate the materials designers should use'.

Only a year later, and facing increasingly disruptive demonstrations, the British Fashion Council officially banned real fur from the catwalks of its fashion weeks. The same cannot be said for fake fur, which is instead being sold to us as an ethical alternative to the needless slaughtering of innocent animals. Fake fur is definitely better for the animals, and for people who abhor wearing dead animals. However, it is well documented that it also carries an unsustainable and questionable impact in its production and disposal phases, as it is made entirely using petroleum, is often produced and manufactured cheaply and unethically (as most cheap things are) and is completely non-biodegradable, therefore ultimately harming numerous other life forms as well as the environment.

FUR CONSEQUENCES

Real fur	Fake fur
☞ Inhumane treatment of animals	☞ Material extraction
☞ Environmental impacts of raising animals	☞ Landfilled waste

You may well decide that, morally, you cannot stomach the unjustified killing of innocent creatures to make a luxury product, and that no fur means *no* fur: real or fake. On the other hand, you may opt to keep wearing real fur, but consider looking for the most ethical options (see overleaf).

BUYING REAL FUR

☞ **Ensure animal welfare**: If you really are going to wear dead animals, ensure you know first how they lived. You'll need to sit down and expiate your desires by looking for the absolute best your money can buy when it comes to animal welfare.

☞ Source from companies that treat animals humanely while they are alive, and that ensure they suffer a pain-free death.

☞ Check that all animals are farmed, and that exotic wildlife is absolutely and rigorously not part of the offering.

☞ Ensure that your fur comes with an 'extended producer guarantee', meaning that whoever made it will share with you the responsibility for its care and eventual disposal.

☞ **Look for fur that is a by-product**: This means that the animal has been farmed and killed for other industry purposes, and its fur is left over in the process. Effectively, your purchase of the hide doesn't fuel this animal's production, but merely makes use of the whole being. Examples include shearling (sheep's hides) and

alpine hares, which are commonly eaten in Switzerland.

☞ **Do not give in to the temptation to buy cheap real fur**: Under no circumstances do this, so avoid all furry pompoms on acrylic hats, and coats with fur-trimmed hoods, which are suspiciously low-cost. Real fur is, and should be, very expensive.

☞ **Switch to vintage**: In my view, this is by far the best option – but again I would ensure buying the utmost quality. As well as looking beautiful for those who love it, a fur coat is a functional product designed to last at least for your for ever, so it must be in good condition and must inspire your commitment to care for it.

☞ **Invest in its maintenance**: In the past, fur coats were made to last for generations, and with them came a whole system designed to look after them. I can clearly remember as a child in Italy fur coats being dispatched for maintenance, just as children would go to holiday camps – taken to some shop to be carefully stored in a cold room during the hot summer months.

Caring for your real fur isn't as easy today, especially with temperatures warming – there's nothing worse for a fur coat than lolling around in a hot wardrobe – and that should be a consideration; put simply, you should buy one only if, as well as having enough money, you also have the willingness to invest in having it professionally maintained.

BUYING FAKE FUR

Fake fur is considerably cheaper than real fur and is often produced in murkier, non-transparent supply chains, so you'll need to be even more vigilant. In some respects, the real-fur industry has been forced to clean up its act, after years of relentless campaigning from animal-rights groups; fake fur, on the other hand, is less scrutinized and the provenance of the raw materials is harder to locate. This means that you will need to pay greater attention to the details, because there will be fewer clues.

There are several things to look out for, when buying fake fur (see overleaf).

☞ **Ingredients**: The best is, if at all possible, a fake-fur piece made from recycled rather than virgin polyester – as with every garment made of polyester. Alternatively, research the best and most innovative alternatives: it will take some time, but considerably less than the 800 years it will take the fake fur that you plan to buy to decompose.

☞ **Colour**: We know that chemicals with proven links to cancers, as well as environmental pollution, such as azo dyes, are used to create the shocking pinks, oranges, limes and fluorescent shades that prevail from high street to high end, so I would choose something more muted instead. Not that beige is free from toxicants by any means, just more likely to be azo dye-free – that's already one less toxic substance in a long list of culprits.

☞ **Quality**: A fake-fur coat needs to be very thoroughly inspected.

☞ How well made is it? Turn it inside out and look at how the lining is sewn: that alone will tell you a lot about the overall make of the piece.

☞ Check that it doesn't shed: badly made fake fur literally comes off if you pull it, and in some cases even if you don't: so get that fur between your fingers, give it a yank and check if it stays put, because fake fur shedding is exactly the same as if you took a plastic bag, cut it into teeny-weeny pieces and blew them into the wind.

☞ **Second-hand items**: Buying second-hand works in the fake-fur case too, and all the same rules apply. Look for quality, buy with love.

The bottom line, when it comes to fur, is that a total rethink is long overdue, because with global warming the likelihood is that very few of us will need it in the first place, so the time is right to switch to kinder materials and kinder aesthetics.

Understanding the fabrics we surround ourselves with is as important, and as beneficial, as knowing the ingredients that we ingest in our food, but it requires a whole new level of learning, digging deep into the minutiae, because these issues are both complex and compelling.

We all need to examine our lifestyles and come up with behavioural changes that will have an impact because we are able to commit to them, to carry them out consistently. If we accept that navigating these choppy waters will take patience and, above all, the effort to make well-informed choices, then the urgency of climate action can be the wind in our sails, with accuracy and knowledge as our masts.

Chapter 6

Denim

Denim is without a doubt one of the most iconic fabrics – if not *the* most iconic fabric – ever made. Yves Saint Laurent famously wished he had invented it, and it has been used by every single designer on Earth in one way or another for decades, from streetwear to haute couture and absolutely everything in between.

This was not intentional: denim was designed to be a durable, affordable fabric for industrial purposes and was originally produced in the French city of Nîmes, hence its name origin '*de Nîmes*', meaning 'from Nîmes'. It was eventually made popular in the USA in the mid-19th century, where its versatile and hard-working properties quickly found use in utility and workwear uniforms, and it wasn't long before the now-ubiquitous denim trousers with reinforced rivets captured the attention of Levi Strauss & Co., which began mass-producing them from their factories in San Francisco around the 1870s.

THE HISTORY

The etymology of the word 'jeans', which we still use today to describe denim trousers, originates from the port from which the denim was shipped: Genoa, in Italy; or Genes, its French name – further proof, as if more were needed, that the geo-location of our materials, their provenance, is woven in their destiny.

Ever since its humble origins, denim has managed to bulldoze its way from niche to mainstream, penetrating and influencing both our culture and our history: a canvas that has become the fabric of so many stories.

Nowadays everyone wears jeans: millionaires, ordinary folk, celebrities, teachers and school kids – jeans are the social climbers that have managed to cross all cultural barriers from workwear to everywhere. They have become, unquestionably, the unanimous trouser of choice, humanity's uniform, a symbol of social and political protest, of unconventionality and individualism.

This rise to global stardom didn't happen overnight. Denim's journey as the 'bad boy' of the textile industry coincided with the turbulent political situation of the early 20th century, and the decline in the rural way of life in favour of a new, mass-operated industrialization, which was simultaneously happening across major global cities. The new 'working class' was born, and immediately exploited, provoking discontent on a global scale, from Russia (where it eventually led to the Russian Revolution of 1917) to Europe and the USA.

What's denim got to do with all this? Well, for the most part it clothed those workers who fuelled the protests; it represented their social standing (or lack thereof), their jobs and their frustrations. Denim dungarees in particular were worn by factory workers and peasants alike – a utilitarian symbol of hard work and daily struggle.

While early fashion theorists discussed the movement of trends as stemming from the wealthy elite and trickling down to the lower classes, the humble uprising of denim represents the opposite journey: from labourers to rebels, and finally to high fashion and catwalks.

How tragic it is to think that this reverse trajectory, which is so closely associated with the start of the workers' rights movement, became a driving force of workers' rights abuses – and workers' safety hazards – by the end of the 20th century.

Jeans further cemented their anti-establishment reputation with the Beat Generation in the 1950s, as worn by generational heroes Jack Kerouac and James Dean – the everyday wear of choice of artists and poets, hobos and rebels – and continued to rise in popular culture throughout the 1960s and '70s, embellished, customized and embroidered to reflect peace and love and all things Flower Power.

Denim raged through the punk movement of the late 1970s, covered in angry black paint and safety pins (and quite a few people actually learned how to sew, just so they could transform their old bell bottoms into Sex Pistol-era super-skinnies), and they ripped their way through the 1980s bleached, fringed and studded.

THE DISTRESSING PROCESS

When I was growing up in the early 1980s, it was Levi's 501s or die. Nick Kamen stripped off to wash them in a launderette; ripped-jeans wearers were banned from Harrods; and teenagers everywhere would spend hours in cold baths to mould them to fit perfectly. If you were an artist they would be splattered in paint; if you were a gardener they would gather earth in their turn-ups. They were never ironed and seldom washed, their durability by design an open invitation to tamper with and personalize.

As we fast-forward to today, the sad irony is that it's precisely this tampering process, which started as a valuable form of self-expression, that has now instead become a monument to all that is wrong with the fashion industry: an expression not of individualism but of speed, impatience and convenience over common sense.

We no longer bother to mess with our own jeans; we'd rather buy a pair that already has someone else's vision imprinted on them. We've run out of patience to let life happen, no longer allowing it to leave its unique fingerprint, made possible only with time. Nowadays it seems that we would rather pay somebody very little money to work in downright dangerous conditions to make it look as though our jeans have character. 'Distressed' denim is the symbol of fast fashion, its most perfect visualization, the physical manifestation of a senseless race to the bottom, with all of its dramatic social and environmental consequences.

It shows how unintelligent, how undesigned it has all become. It shows how, for the sake of looking exactly the same as everybody else, we are compromising on who we are as individuals, and compromising on the well-being of our planet and the people who make our clothes.

By his own admission in the film *RiverBlue*, it was François Girbaud who first used chemicals and other intrusive methods such as sandblasting, stone-washing and the use of corrosive acids to turn denim – a strong, durable and seemingly indestructible material that would take years to distress naturally – into an overnight sensation of a life not really lived. This initiated a trend that eventually led to, and is still responsible for, gross environmental degradation, as well as considerable health hazards for those involved in its production. If ever there was a 'killer look', distressed denim would be it, quite literally.

'We make a mistake at the beginning, we were responsible. When we start first, we don't realize how what we did was wrong . . . I tried to find everything more crazy, we make all this treatment, washing, all the process of washing, we invent from 1972 to 1989. We continue invention, using everything, acid, etc., etc. But I realized the importance of our work. What we did, what was the reaction. Because pollution of river, everything, we invent that.'

François Girbaud, designer

The fact is, denim really took off, and artificially distressed denim – this senseless, highly damaging trend – has become inescapable for more than 40 years. And despite the recent push towards innovative and sustainable solutions, when it comes to our (not so blue) jeans, much of the damage has already been done.

Of all the methods developed to distress denim, sandblasting is among the most harmful and life-threatening techniques. Widely used to achieve the 'worn' look, it relies on abrasive materials, such as sand particles that are blasted onto the denim with a machine by workers – who are typically exposed and unprotected – to soften the fabric and lighten the characteristic dark-indigo dye, which in turn makes jeans look as though they have been loved and worn and washed a million times. For well over 60 years this technique has been common practice in denim production and has shockingly claimed many lives, due to its direct link with the condition silicosis, a deadly respiratory disease caused by the inhalation of tiny particles of silica. These are invisible to the naked eye and gradually impair lung capacity, causing shortness of breath and putting strain on the heart.

Originally used in mining, not fashion, sandblasting was banned by the European Economic Community in 1966. However, the ban didn't come into effect in Turkey (one of the biggest denim-producing countries) until 2009. Sandblasting is still legal, and practised (albeit not so openly), in many other countries. Essentially it is up to the brands themselves to ensure that this harmful technique is rendered obsolete in our supply chain; and many companies – among which are numerous household names, from the high street and the high end alike – are caught offending on a regular basis.

Even without sandblasting, many of the methods still in use in denim factories cannot be considered environmentally-friendly. I visited one such factory in Sri Lanka in 2008 and it was gold-standard, meaning best in practice, producing for some of the best-known denim brands in the world. At the time of my visit, distressed denim was at the height of its trendiness, and you practically couldn't find a pair of regular dark-blue jeans without rips or tears or distressing of one kind or another.

The atmosphere in this 'gold-standard' factory was unbearable – the dizzying smell of unidentified chemical fumes, the required 98 per cent humidity, the denim dust and human sweat permeated everything. Although, as visitors on the factory tour (which included several fashion-industry practitioners), we were provided with masks, I noticed that none of the workers wore one, and even wearing one myself, within 20 minutes my throat was itchy.

Although steps had been taken to equip the factory with all the latest innovation, when an entire system is geared towards artificially stripping a very resilient fabric of all its strength as quickly as possible, the dispensable use of water, chemicals and insanity is visible for all to see. As with many things 'fashion', if it wasn't so tragic, it might be classified as comedy . . .

I saw lines upon lines of workers furiously scrubbing the bums of denim-clad mannequins hanging from the ceiling with sandpaper brushes; others carefully applying fake creases at anatomical points of the trousers that would otherwise never crease naturally; other workers perennially wet from moving materials from one disgusting sludge-bath to the next.

Naively, I had assumed that this sector of the industry might be less wasteful, more capable to include (or hide) in their final deliveries imperfect runs, which would normally be discarded immediately for brand-protection purposes. Logic told me that a rip is a rip, after all, and tears come in all shapes and sizes, and I never imagined that there would be garment workers, armed with measuring tapes and magnifying glasses, employed exclusively to check that all imperfections are perfect, as each brand has its own strict rules about what kind of damage they specifically want, and exactly where it should occur. When you see these identical distressing processes repeated across millions of pieces (because these manufacturers deliver millions of pairs of jeans on a weekly basis), it starts to look truly crazy.

The madness of this was not lost on the factory workers, who meticulously reclaimed as much wasted material as possible for their own use and had devised a brilliant 'interior decor' of their workplace, using discarded denim scraps to make tool bags, covers for wooden stools and sewing machines, and cushions to be used in the canteen. As a result, the factory's communal spaces looked like something out of a loft conversion in New York and wouldn't have been out of place among the pages of a high-end interiors magazine.

As consumers, we may well have become immune or desensitized to surplus and waste, but for those who see it every day – for those who work in systems (such as clothing factories) where waste that isn't really waste is generated and discarded in a constant cycle – the incumbency, the weight of it, is heavy, both practically and emotionally. For many garment workers, or at least many that I have spoken with, the way we waste is as incomprehensible as it is abominable. I see it as a metaphorical slap in the face of common sense; an affront to poverty, when a perfectly good resource is thrown away for the sake of a frantic production rhythm that benefits absolutely nobody, apart from the few individuals at the top of a very toxic hierarchy.

It takes four days for a major fashion CEO to earn what a female garment worker in Bangladesh will earn in her entire lifetime, according to Oxfam's *Reward Work, Not Wealth* paper of January 2018.

THE GAME

I have been playing a game with myself when it comes to jeans for the best part of the last ten years. I haven't given it a name (yet), but it consists of trying to analyse the artificial wear-and-tear on factory-distressed jeans and imagine what kind of life the wearers of those jeans would have had, in order to incur that kind of damage and distressing naturally. It all started on a flight back from Italy in the late Naughties, with the guy who was sitting next to me . . .

He was what we would then have called 'metrosexual', doused in the smell of clashing deodorant, aftershave and scent, with an immaculately trimmed beard and sideburns, all unruly facial hair expertly razored, except for a tiny dark pathway on a sea of impeccably moisturized pink skin; his white shirt ironed to perfection, polished designer shoes, and all the rest. His whole persona screamed of grooming, cleanliness and control. And then there were his jeans.

Analysing his jeans anatomically – according to The Game – I concluded that he must have spent quite a bit of time rubbing his thighs with something rough. At one point he might have been mauled by a dog that bit his right leg, or perhaps he stumbled upon some sharp object; but he was good at sewing, or his mum was, because he bothered to patch the rip up.

But the main, and most disconcerting, element of the jeans' inauthentic distressing were tiny whiskers ('whiskers' is, believe it or not, the technical term to describe the fake creases that are painted on denim to make them look wrinkled and worn), in particular around the groin area and the back of the knees – and that kind of use could only happen to someone who had spent an inordinate amount of time wearing their pants all the way down. Like 25 years on the toilet, for example. It was a bit contradictory, considering how neat and careful this person was about his looks, to imagine that he'd be happy to tell us – quite openly, via the trousers he wore – that he had been suffering from such a prolonged and severe case of diarrhoea! Ever since, I have progressed to identify several distress designs that tell the story of some distinctly eccentric life choices, or terrible illnesses.

If you collected together a whole bunch of pre-distressed denim pieces from our generation, put them in a box and left them, say, 10,000 years (and the reason you are reading this book, BTW, is because you want to help ensure that humans will be alive in 10,000 years' time), any future anthropologist looking at them would conclude that humans at the turn of the 21st century were doing all sorts of really weird stuff, according to how they 'wore out' their jeans: hours rubbing our bums on rough surfaces; crawling constantly; wearing trousers down instead of up; accidentally misusing acid; having violent tussles with wild animals on a regular basis; and probably suffering from regular episodes of urticaria, in particular on the shins and thighs.

'Ridiculous' may not be a strong enough word to describe this phenomenon, but it is nevertheless worthy of all our ridicule, because for these absurd-looking jeans (like millions of other pairs of jeans), the point is not just how much we are prepared to compromise in order to own them – such as in respect for the people who made them (cheap jeans = cheap labour) and the environmental footprint they come laden with – but how blissfully stupid we are prepared to look when we wear them. Let me tell you right now: there is no joy in owning jeans like these.

Still, demand for denim is increasing exponentially every year: incredibly, in 2017 alone we produced globally more than 1.95 billion pairs of jeans. According to Lyst, the world's largest fashion search platform, jeans are one of the world's most-searched-for fashion items, with an average of 13 searches per second, and approximately 1,240,000,000 pairs of jeans are sold worldwide every year. In 2019 searches for 'sustainable denim' increased 193 per cent, to become one of the top three key words when searching for sustainable fashion.

Luckily, passing trends (at the time of writing, dark-blue jeans are firmly back in fashion) and an increased awareness of the negative impact of the fashion industry are generating demand for responsible solutions, and the denim industry has been quick to respond, placing itself at the very forefront of the conversation about innovation and sustainability.

INNOVATION

Advances in technology, when it comes to the production and distressing of denim, are growing exponentially, and there are several new techniques being touted as cleaner, greener and more sustainable. Look for:

- ☞ **Laser technology** (less-intensive labour, less use of chemicals)
- ☞ **Foam dyeing** (using air instead of water to carry dyes onto the yarns, with fewer chemicals)
- ☞ **Ozone processing** (used for a gentler, less abrasive fading effect)
- ☞ **Nitrogen dyeing** (slowing down oxidation and facilitating the process of dyes' yarn penetration)
- ☞ **Hydrite denim** (which promises a 95 per cent reduction in water use)
- ☞ **OrganIQ Bleach** (an alternative to the use of potassium permanganate, which was previously considered safer, but is now in question)
- ☞ **Surface activation** (a more ethical and sustainable alternative to sandblasting).

The denim companies that are positively innovating will definitely want their customers to know they are, and will market their sustainability efforts on the products they sell; you should be able to identify quite easily the brands and products that are committed to better practices within the industry.

Mohsin Sajid, Creative Director of ENDRIME and Educational Denim Platform: Denim History, is one of the world's most influential denim experts, and he told me that in the current denim-making business – from growing cotton, or making polyester from petrochemicals, weaving to sewing, and finally garment finishing – nearly every aspect of denim production uses vast amounts of water and harmful or poisonous chemicals to bleach and break down the jean fabric and discolour the indigo colour.

The main ingredient in chemical indigo, which is currently most used throughout the world, is benzene, which is rat poison.

The push for innovation over the past few years has been looking at alternatives to cotton, polyester and chemical indigo, to try and reduce water usage – or keep it in a closed-loop system so that it does not affect the surrounding areas of production. Mohsin suggests checking out:

☞ **Coreva Stretch Technology**: A new natural, rubber fibre patented by the Italian denim mill Candiani. It's 'bio-stretch' and will break down in a landfill and not shed microplastics in the environment – it's pure innovation – which will change this planet, if adopted by all mills.

☞ **TENCEL™ x Candiani**: A 2019 ITMA Sustainable Innovation award-winning fabric, which is a 50/50 blend of TENCEL™ x REFIBRA™ Lyocell and recycled cotton. Absolutely no virgin cotton is used – and it's considered the most advanced denim fabric produced to date.

☞ **Tinctorium Inc.'s Greener Indigo Solution**: Conventional indigo dyeing requires large amounts of harmful chemicals to break down the compounds and dissolve the pigment in water. Tinctorium has replaced this chemical process with bacteria. This is currently being scaled up, and it's looking very promising.

☞ **Hemp denim**: Apparently most denim mills are experimenting or already blending hemp, as it produces twice as much fibre per land area compared to cotton.

BUYING DENIM

☞ **Buy recycled:** Look for brands that incorporate recycled fibres, such as recycled cotton or other recycled post-consumer waste: replacing 20 per cent of the cotton in denim with recycled materials can save up to 500 litres of water per garment in the production phase, and addresses the waste problem at the same time.

☞ **Buy vintage:** Why buy new ripped jeans if you can buy the real thing? Old jeans? I rest my case.

☞ **Upcycle your old denim:** Denim lends itself to all kinds of transformative creative processes, allowing itself to be thoroughly redesigned and reinterpreted into new products before it finally becomes waste. There is more on upcycling in Chapter 7, but for now here are a few ideas to get you started:

> ☞ I will never understand people who buy denim shorts (and that includes my daughters). Why? Why can't you just cut down the ones you already own?
> ☞ I have seen denim pockets become almost anything, from the cutest phone pouches (join two pockets together and add a long strap – this could be beaded, sequinned, crocheted, woven, knitted or customized) to advent calendars!
> ☞ Keep your old jeans to patch your new ones.
> ☞ The robust material also lends itself to household duties: I use my kids' old jeans to polish silver and brass, and someone I know has made the best-ever pot holders, simply by layering two squares and binding them together with crochet.

HOW TO TURN YOUR OLD JEANS INTO A SKIRT

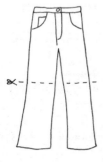

1.
Lay out your jeans and cut across the legs at the point you want your skirt to end, plus an extra couple of centimetres for the hem.

2.
Use a seam-ripper to unpick the inseam of your trouser legs. You'll also need to unpick the crotch seam until just below the fly on the front and about the middle of the bum at the back.

3.
With the front of the jeans facing you, flatten out the unpicked crotch seam so that one side overlaps the other. Pin and then stitch this into place (you can follow the original stitching line as a guide), folding over the raw inseam edge to neaten (or not – leave it raw!). Repeat this for the crotch seam on the back of your jeans.

4.
Now you need to fill in the triangular gap between the legs with a scrap panel from the bottom part of the jeans that you cut away. You could choose a contrasting fabric for this bit – up to you! Slip a panel of fabric behind the gap, pin it into place and stitch down both sides of the inseam to secure.

5.
Trim off any excess at the hem, and either leave it raw or fold and press it to the inside and top-stitch it down.

CARING FOR DENIM

☞ **Wash less:** Washing a pair of jeans every ten times you wear them instead of every other time reduces energy use, climate-change impact and water intake by up to 80 per cent.

☞ **Keep them on rotation:** Most people (who can afford it) own several pairs of jeans, it really isn't all that difficult to use them in rotation and refresh them. Ways to refresh your jeans:

> ☞ Spot-clean and sponge them, as described in Chapter 4.
> ☞ Shove them in the freezer or steam them in between washes (see pages 77 and 74).

As well as possessing durability and longevity by design, denim has another property that makes it right for reuse – its sheer abundance. Because there is so much denim on this planet, and because it takes on a repetitive aesthetic, denim is perfect for upcycling – a fact not lost on a new generation of creatives who are specializing in bringing it back to life.

We will look at this in detail in the next chapter, but for now let's celebrate this miracle material as a success story, the fabric of our modern society – the one cloth that has had the power to become a form of political expression and capture our imagination like no other.

DISTRESS YOUR OWN DENIM

☞ You will need: scissors for cutting, tweezers for fringing, needle and thread for embroidery and stitching, sandpaper or a cheese grater to roughen up the texture, paints and brushes for splatters and doodles, a sponge and bleach for the 1980s stonewash effect, patches (made of crochet, knitted or from old materials), a little bit of time and not that much imagination. Experiment with any or all of the things above and see how creative you can get. ✌

Chapter 7

My Trash

When it comes to fashion textiles and clothes, trash is my favourite subject: I know too much about it for my own good. I wear it, I work with it, I lecture about it, I know where it occurs and where it ends up and I know how to avoid it. They don't call me the 'Queen of Upcycling' for no reason!

To love fashion, and to appreciate it for its multiple functions, includes changing our mindset and considering clothing end-of-life as a top priority, because the only way to halt the disastrous effects of our modern-day attitude towards disposability is to question what is rubbish in the first place, and to think about the *longevity* of our clothing – and its efficient usage – in order to prolong its life for as long as possible.

We need to mend, repair and rewear, not just as individuals, but systematically, as a society. Clothing end-of-life should be a shared responsibility, with brands being responsible for producing clothes that are durable and recyclable; local governments being responsible for providing adequate and readily available recycling facilities, supporting local infrastructures to include repairing as a high-street standard; and citizens being responsible for buying sensibly and looking after their clothes, as well as engaging in activities such as swapping and renting, to actively prevent accelerated disposal.

THE JOURNEY

When I was growing up, and until relatively recently, donating clothes to charity was an act of goodwill: unwanted clothes would either be diverted directly to families in need or sold in charity shops. People donated sparingly and carefully, but safe in the knowledge that their surplus really did go to a good cause.

One of the first charity shops in the UK was opened by the Wolverhampton Society for the Blind (now called the Beacon Centre for the Blind) as far back as 1899, while Oxfam, the organization for the relief of world poverty, opened its first UK store in 1948. Charity shops operate a system of reselling the best crop of donated clothing for a premium price in their retail stores to finance their humanitarian operations, and selling the 'rags' (items that should be so used, so worn, so broken that they are not deemed worthy of the shop front) to textile traders, who further sell them on to developing countries or for fibre-to-fibre recycling.

In the USA, UK and Canada, charities sell anything from 10 to 30 per cent of donated clothes in their stores, and the rest is sold in bulk to textile sorting and recycling companies, who export the vast majority. Globally, 70 per cent of donated clothes end up in Africa, according to *The Guardian* in 2015, but they are also sent to other countries such as Haiti or to Eastern Europe.

Once exported to developing countries, our clothes wreak havoc with local economies and infrastructures and are in part responsible for the widespread demise of local artisanal industries, which cannot compete with their low prices, or with the fact that Western clothes are seen as being more aspirational and fashionable than local textile crafts and traditional clothing.

In Ghana second-hand clothes that arrive in the country have been nicknamed '*Obroni Wawu*', which roughly translates as 'dead white man's clothes'. It's a telling folklore about an excess of clothes, and Liz Ricketts and J. Branson Skinner, of the research project entitled 'Dead White Man's Clothes', estimate that a staggering 15 million items flow through the Accra markets each week. 'Although nearly everyone dealing in second-hand

70 per cent of clothes donated to charity shops are _sold in bulk_ to textile sorting companies.

clothes today knows that most of the clothing is originally given away by people who are still alive, we think that this concept of Dead White Man's Clothes speaks to the absurdity of the waste that we, a society, create as a by-product of our exploitative over-consumption and over-production,' say the project founders (https://deadwhitemansclothes.org/intro).

According to Oxfam, importing second-hand clothes costs the African economy an average of US $42.5 million a year, a sum that could instead be invested in maintaining and supporting local textile and craft infrastructures. David Woode, a Ghanaian-born, UK-based journalist, speaks of the influx of second-hand clothing as a detriment to local industry:

'In Britain, custom-made clothing is seen as a preserve of the rich, but in Ghana it's very much a part of the fabric of life . . . Of course, there's no escaping how second-hand clothing in Ghana has decimated the local textile economy.

But for tailors, seamstresses and printmakers, it's presented an opportunity to not only create clothes that people desire – and ones they will treasure – but make use of the traditional skills and craftsmanship passed down to them by relatives and tutors and secure their futures.'

[David Woode]

That our cheap, unwanted, readily discarded fashion is making redundant the use of beautiful local cloth and costume is, to my mind, one of the greatest cultural disasters we have ever witnessed, on a par with burning books, or the destruction of ancient pottery during the Cultural Revolution in China. Western clothes may be cheaper to buy and seen as trendier than local craft offerings, but their cultural and environmental cost far outweighs any real benefit for local consumers.

OUR TRASH:
POST-CONSUMER WASTE

Post-consumer waste is all waste that derives from us, starting with when we bought it and it left the store. Post-consumer waste adequately recycled (disposed of in textile facilities or donated to charity) is recovered and sold locally or overseas. The remainder is 'downcycled' into lower-value products (such as fillings for mattresses, wipes, carpet underlay and car insulation).

Everything that you throw away carelessly without a strategy for its disposal – even if you do what is perceived to be the 'good' option and you take it to a charity shop – is of consequence. Perhaps you bought it as carelessly as you are prepared to throw it away. But maybe, after reading about its end-of-life impact, you will decide to keep it.

Global figures make for uncomfortable reading (especially as many of us are guilty as charged):

53 PER CENT OF 1,000 PEOPLE POLLED IN HONG KONG REVEALED THAT THEY OWNED CLOTHES THAT WERE STILL TAGGED, COMPARED WITH 51 PER CENT IN MAINLAND CHINA, 46 PER CENT IN ITALY, 41 PER CENT IN GERMANY AND 40 PER CENT IN TAIWAN.

ACCORDING TO OXFAM, 2+ TONNES OF CLOTHING ARE BOUGHT EACH MINUTE IN THE UK, AND EACH WEEK 11 MILLION GARMENTS END UP IN LANDFILL.

NEW YORKERS THROW 200,000,000,000 LBS OF CLOTHING INTO THE TRASH EVERY YEAR. THAT'S THE EQUIVALENT OF 440 STATUES OF LIBERTY.

Charity shops are full to the brim, mostly with clothes that were so cheap in the first place that it seems pointless to discount them any further; and those rags that I mentioned previously are now, more often than not, in exactly the same state as the clothes that reach the shop floor: cheap, unworn, unloved, abandoned.

Needless to say, invading others with what we can't get rid of ourselves is no guarantee of accurate disposal processes, because many of the countries that receive our surplus are ill-equipped to manage the load; clothes are subsequently dumped in local land-fills or end up scattered on the streets – a shameful visual display of a system that has lost control. There simply is no more space for all these unwanted clothes – not in our wardrobes or in our world. That is why we need to recycle clothes responsibly and not chuck them out in household bins, or donate to charity without having considered other available options, like mending, reselling or swapping instead.

THE CLEAR-OUT

When it comes to clothes, deciding where they will end up is as important as knowing where they come from. So stop right here for a moment and take a tour of your wardrobe. Check in with your clothes, especially those that have been neglected and those already earmarked for the charity bin. As you slowly leaf through your dresses, shirts, trousers and skirts, ask yourself:

DO I STILL LOVE IT?
Does it fit me well? Is it too 'last season'?

IS IT IN GOOD CONDITION? IF SO:
Could I sell it on?
Could it be donated to a homeless shelter or to charity? Find out what your local homeless shelter actually needs before offloading your clothes.
Could I gift it to a friend or neighbour? I often put a rail of my unwanted clothes outside my front door, so that friends, neighbours and passers-by can help themselves.

IS IT BROKEN OR DAMAGED? IF SO:
Could I repair it, customize it, rework or reclaim it, instead of getting rid of it?
Could I DIY it? Or do I know someone who can?
Could it be repurposed into something else completely?

WHAT HAPPENS WHEN I THROW MY CLOTHES AWAY?

To determine clothes' sell-by date, we need to understand the materials they are made from – whether they are natural, in which case they will biodegrade faster; or synthetic, in which case their presence on the Earth will outlive their wearer by a significantly long time.

ROUGHLY HOW LONG DO CLOTHES TAKE TO BIODEGRADE IN LANDFILL?

That said, biodegradation and composting fabric have their toxic effects too, because all clothes in landfill release methane gas as they decompose – the infamous cow-fart substance that is the dreaded culprit of global heating. Most clothes, even if made with natural and biodegradable materials, are usually sewn with polyester thread and contain all kinds of added components, such as synthetic labels, plastic buttons and zips; elements that are often made using metals that are unethically mined and brimming with toxicants.

Linen shirt
2 weeks

Polyester dress
200 years, minimum

Viscose T-shirt
1–6 weeks

Lycra activewear
20–200 years

Wool jumper
1–5 years

As an example, the belief that wool is biodegradable and will decompose in a matter of weeks is an entirely mythical idea, when the treatment of modern materials is factored in. If you sheared a sheep and left its wool in the compost pile, it would decompose along with all the other organic matter that we consider biodegradable. Due to the volume of nitrogen in animal hairs, it would even leave behind beneficial nutrients for the soil. But textile wool – cleaned and scoured, carded and spun, dyed and woven, and then finished with anything from antistatic agents to flame retardants – is far from compostable. And in its toxic state, when thrown away, wool also releases methane gas into the soil as its chemical journey breaks it down.

Biodegradable is definitely better than non-biodegradable; however, clothes should be designed to be worn, not buried or burned.

Denim jacket
10–12 months

Cotton socks
1 week–5 months

Silk camisole
1–3 years

Nylon tights
30–40 years

THEIR TRASH: PRE-CONSUMER WASTE

Pre-consumer waste is all leftover materials from clothing production throughout the supply chain – everything from the spinning of yarns to the sewing of the garments. Pre-consumer waste is divided into two types:

☞ **Fabric waste**: anything from cutting-room-floor offcuts to damaged rolls of fabric, end of rolls and other pre-production leftovers.

☞ **Clothing waste**: such as dead stock (that's unsold garments), damaged runs (clothing that is considered defective at production level) and cancelled orders (brands will always order 10 per cent extra, in case the item is successful and store stock needs to be replenished quickly), fully or part-made, and other post-production surplus.

It is estimated that a single textile mill will waste 5–25 per cent of pre-consumer textiles of its total yearly production, while manufacturers on average will waste approximately 15 per cent of production offcuts alone.

The problem of disposability and waste is one that will define generations to come, as they will bear the ultimate responsibility for cleaning up the mess we made in a few destructive, blind decades, during which we have systematically produced too much of everything, in a linear way, without considering the effects of this man-centric, nature-denying model of unrestrained growth.

Astonishingly, and I am quoting Christina Dean, founder and CEO of Redress, a Hong Kong charity organization that looks at clothing waste and ways to recuperate at scale:

75 per cent of apparel purchases are made at discounted prices – fuelling a race to the bottom where increasingly lower price points get consumers hooked on cheap, cheap, cheap! Some traditional retailers now have more discount outlets than full-price stores. But when the thrill of discounted shopping fails to entice the consumer into making a purchase, then brands and retailers must get rid of their 'dead stock'. The truth is that offering discounted prices will never ensure that all products are sold. Retail space, warehouse space and even prime website ad-space isn't infinite, which means products that aren't selling need to be gotten rid of. But where?

The present system couldn't be less transparent or more malfunctioning, and although we are just beginning to understand what happens to our discarded clothing – thanks to several reports published in recent years, driven by an increased interest in this subject – we still have very little information about what is discarded at source, in the fashion supply chain, during the various production phases.

What we do know is that, as with almost every other aspect in fashion production, little attention is being paid to efficiency, common sense and resources, whether natural or man-made; we discard with aplomb at every single level of the value chain, burning and destroying stock and fabrics as the norm.

In many cases, big brands' legal requirements demand that, if a garment run comes out wrong or a fabric is damaged, it must be destroyed in the interest of brand protection: this can be through slashing and then disposal, via incineration or landfill.

In July 2018 Burberry announced that it had burned US \$50 million worth of clothes and accessories in the name of 'brand protection', a story that incensed the media and consumers alike when it broke, and took almost a full month to die down. What became increasingly interesting as it progressed (and I was one of the experts called into question by the international press) was that it was the first time this issue reached the public, when in fact it is an open secret and a regular practice in the fashion industry.

There had been previous scandals involving H&M incinerating clothes, Nike slashing unworn sneakers, and Cartier destroying unsold watches, but the Burberry moment was the first time that consumers and the media really took notice and understood the implications, albeit with much disbelief.

Because all big brands burn: they burn samples they can't store; their mills burn millions of metres of fabrics from past seasons that have logos or identifiable patterns; their manufacturers burn damaged runs; and their retailers burn unsold stock and returns.

It doesn't take a mathematical genius to work it out: we produce approximately 150 billion garments of clothing (not counting shoes and accessories) every year, and there are 7.7 billion of us; inevitably, a huge proportion of clothes won't ever reach their customers, being nonsensically designed to be disposed of.

What I learned from the Burberry burning story was that it ignited more consumer outrage than the collapse of the Rana Plaza factory complex, and that people who had somewhat failed to identify with, or feel empathy for, the plight of supply-chain workers and their potentially deadly working conditions found it utterly unacceptable and disrespectful that brands should so carelessly dispose of those same products that their hard-earned money goes to buy. The things we choose and value have no value at all for the brands that produce them.

RECYCLING
OPTIONS

MECHANICAL RECYCLING

The current waste problem is a direct result of mass production and over-consumption and, therefore, a relatively modern phenomenon. In the not-so-distant past, mills and factories were run much more effectively and the reuse of old stock and remnants (as well as the mechanical recycling of offcuts and cutting-room-floor waste) was integrated into everyday practices.

Single-fibre materials, such as wool and cotton, were recuperated at scale and returned to new life as yarns, their quality slightly compromised, but recycling facilities were widespread wherever there was textile production.

Downcycling is still comparatively common in the textile industry – and by 'downcycling' we mean the shredding and re-pulping of offcuts and production waste to make wet-wipes, mattress filling, car insulation, low-quality yarns and other textiles – and provides a viable, sustainable alternative to landfill and incineration.

However, reintroducing fibres of the kind of high quality we need in order to make further fashion products is not so easy in today's world, and mechanical recycling, once a thriving, efficient industry existing alongside most fashion and textile manufacturing, almost disappeared – another victim of speed and convenience.

The reason why we can't recycle as much as we used to is simple: we have complicated clothing materials in our efforts to cheapen them, and have consequently made them much more difficult to recycle. One hundred per cent wool and 100 per cent cotton – even 100 per cent polyester – are less-common composition labels on the high street; our jumpers are widely 80 per cent acrylic/20 per cent wool, our jeans are now 97 per cent cotton/3 per cent elastane, and our T-shirts are increasingly cotton with a splash of polyester. These blended fibres, designed to mimic their more expensive pure materials, are materials that we do not (yet) have the technology to separate and recycle.

CHEMICAL RECYCLING

'The potential for circularity in clothing and apparel, where raw materials are kept in continual circulation, is completely achievable yet the barriers preventing it are challenging,' says Cyndi Rhoades (https://circularlondon.org/fashion/), Founder of Worn Again Technologies, a pioneering organization that has been working on the concept of chemical recycling for eight years and has just opened the first UK chemical-recycling pilot facility for turning polyester and cotton to cellulose.

While mechanical recycling involves the shredding and re-spinning of fibres, chemical recycling is a more complex process. Relatively new, and still in its infancy of development, chemical recycling and circular systems, in the case of polyester, break textiles down to polymers or monomers. Depending on how much you remember of high-school chemistry, this effectively means that molecules that have bonded together to form plastic fibres can be broken down and stripped of contaminants, to be built up again and made into new materials.

In theory, this circular process could bring mixed fibres back to equal-quality raw materials that can be reused to keep making clothes, for ever.

We know that we can recycle polyester by burning it down, because that's all you can do to plastic. We know that we can recuperate single fibres with effective mechanical recycling; chemical recycling represents the final frontier – the possibility that one day soon we will be able to effectively recycle all fibres (pure or blends) into any yarn, using our unworn clothes as the raw material to feed the loop, and all will be well again.

Except, unfortunately, not quite. Right now this is a theory, and not yet a practice, and we are still mass-producing like crazy; so what are we doing with all that stuff in the meantime? I hope, but somehow doubt, that brands will go mining landfills once they have the technology to recycle properly, purely to lessen the burden. But wouldn't it make more sense to slow down production now, while we invest in circularity, rather than keep making in order to throw?

As a consumer, you too have the power to slow down the industry, by making precise and well-conceived decisions about how you care for your clothes, and by questioning what prompts you to buy them in the first place.

The truth is that we are far from implementing efficient and clean chemical-recycling systems that will turn discarded fabrics into reuseable fibres – we are progressing, but slowly, compared to how fast we are producing. Furthermore, recycling and closed-loop technologies should only be considered as an end solution, with the prerogative being to produce an adequate amount of well-made, eco-designed, fully recyclable clothes, made from low-impact materials by people in well-paid jobs, not as an excuse to keep going the way we are now.

Because even if, or when, we are able to recycle fully in a functioning closed-loop system, the fact remains that any system that is based on producing excessive volumes will still generate an incredibly heavy environmental toll.

One final word of advice: circular means full-circle, from fibre back to fibre, and the capability of repeating this process ad infinitum. Wearing vintage, buying second-hand, swapping, renting, upcycling – none of that is circular. That's longevity, efficiency and care, which is equally important (if not more important), because, as consumers, that's where we can truly have a sizeable impact.

THE CASE FOR UPCYCLING

Upcycling is a creative design solution to an environmental challenge, encompassing aesthetics, technique, problem-solving and worshipping at the altar of creative thinking, efficiency and common sense.

There is a kind of poetry in taking the unwanted and giving it another life, and upcycling as a design process has its own visual signature, its own set of values and its own unique methods. It may not be for everyone, but those who love it can become passionately addicted. It encourages time – the single most undervalued word in fashion's modern history – and patience, which, along with time, is part of an ancient fashion lexicon. It encourages a journey of discovery whereby the sources of fashion waste are located, materials are 'saved' and reintroduced into the system via the intelligent use of design and skills. (Or you can read it as: find the trash, pack it into the back of your van, take it to your studio and sew it into something amazing.)

Upcycling may be a new definition – it was first coined by Reiner Pilz in 1994: 'Recycling,' he said, 'I call it downcycling. They smash bricks, they smash everything. What we need is upcycling – where old products are given more value, not less' (https://www.commonobjective.co/article/the-creativity-of-upcycling-design-solution-for-the-planet). So the name may be new, but as we have been 'upcycling' for millennia in all forms of crafts, art and design, the concept is embedded in our DNA. I bring you back to *boro*, quilting and *kintsugi* (see Chapter 2).

However, it is often difficult to understand the difference between recycling and upcycling, especially as we are now recuperating fibres in so many ways and from so many sources (indeed, the transformation of a discarded water bottle into further polyester yarn, or the conversion of fishing nets into fabrics, increases their properties – and their value – rather than diminishing them). But in my opinion, the difference between the two isn't just in the quality of the fibres, but in the way they are produced, using creativity as the measure: upcycling, to my mind, is about recuperating materials without the intervention of any further chemical or mechanical processes.

So whereas 'recycling' is turning fibre back into fibre, 'upcycling' is turning cloth (or clothes) into new clothes.

Although teaching upcycling in universities is on the increase, it is by no means embedded in the curriculum, and although students are increasingly being taught zero-waste pattern-cutting as a technique, attention to surplus and its use is not as widely considered as it could be; from the onset of their studies, fashion and textile students (as well as any student making any kind of product) should be taught how to minimize waste throughout their education, and how to value it as a resource.

When it comes to the industry, we could be creating new positions, such as trained 'waste engineers', inside both brands' and manufacturers' sourcing and production departments, whose responsibility should be knowing where the surplus is kept, whether it is dead-stock fabric, damaged fabrics, unsold clothes or defective runs; they should know which types of waste are re-useable and how to offer it to their clients to reincorporate in their collections.

There should be upcycling facilities in factories, ready to produce new stuff from whatever is deemed unuseable (like the objects I described made in the denim factory in Sri Lanka, see page 133), and garment workers should be taught disassembling and reassembling, as a way to decrease waste and increase their skill sets.

Just like the materials that are reused, this is nothing new – it has been done before, plenty of times, and the knowledge is there. It has been done as a result of poverty and need (there are stories of women scouring textile factories collecting off-cuts for clothes-making during wartime), and it has been done consistently in the past by the fashion industry to maximize efficiency. Couture always/regularly upcycles, its precious fabric scraps being too expensive to go to waste. And nowadays upcycling is increasingly being used by design pioneers who see it as a creative and practical way to antagonize mass production and mass consumption.

Waste is a design flaw, as well as a design resource. We need to develop a 360-degree design vision, where every bit of everything made is reuseable, adaptable or recyclable. We already have enough plastics and textiles corrupting our environment, and we now need a closed-loop vision for an open-minded future.

So while we wait for technology to save us, why not upscale upcycling instead? It's one of the best bets we've got to still make wonderful clothes while slowing down the fashion industry. As resources become scarcer and more expensive, as the issue of fashion and textile waste drowning the planet becomes more obvious, following a global call for brand transparency (which will finally allow for a detailed mapping of where, when and how much waste occurs at every point in the supply chain), what we are looking at is a viable alternative: one that will be creating new skills and new jobs, and will move us towards an efficient industry where surplus is addressed long before it becomes waste.

UPCYCLING DESIGNERS

When I started writing this book I swore to myself that I wasn't going to mention any designers. This is because the lifespan of a young designer can be so brief these days, and I didn't want to run the risk of mentioning anyone who could have gone out of business by the time this book was in print. My brand was included in so many publications, always in the present tense, making many wonderful books completely out of date from 2014, when we closed. Yet supporting emerging talents is what I do (and very little has made me as proud in my career as to be called 'Fashion Mum' by some of them), and I have so much respect for some of the pioneers in my community, that I decided I will at the very least name some who I think will be remembered – people who have tried to change something along the way, and who will be indelible in the minds of those who come after them.

Some of these designers I have known since London Fashion Week's Estethica days, and many are part of the Fashion Revolution's Fashion Open Studio initiative, curated by fellow revolutionary and longtime fashion journalist Tamsin Blanchard. They all have stories to tell that will stay etched in time. Find them, support them: they deserve your full attention.

CHRISTOPHER RAEBURN – the original pioneer of the present generation of upcyclists and someone who has beautifully integrated the endemic reuse of waste in all his practice.

DURAN LANTINK – who juxtaposes different designers' unsold work into iconoclastic pieces that question 'brand protection' practices, using upcycling as a potential overstock problem-solver.

PRIYA AHLUWALIA – who reuses second-hand and pre-loved items at scale by introducing them in her sportswear-inspired collections.

KEVIN GERMANIER – who dresses all the top celebrities, such as Lady Gaga, Taylor Swift and Kristen Stewart, in upcycled jeans and dead-stock fabrics intricately embellished with broken and discarded beading.

HELEN KIRKUM – who upcycles old trainers into trainer couture.

And there are others all over the world: Angus Tsui in Hong Kong, Doodlage and Iro Iro in India, the brilliant Soup Archive in Berlin, and many, many more (you'll find a larger list in the Further Reading section of this book, see page 236).

One special mention goes to Bethany Williams, someone for whom I nurture a deep respect and have the pleasure of being at the end of the phone. For her beautiful collections, Bethany upcycles existing materials – denim in particular – or chooses virgin fabrics that are sustainably made, incorporating traditional crafts such as hand-weaving and hand-knitting. But what makes her unique are her collaborations: each season she will be inspired by a local charitable organization (such as the Quaker Mobile Library, the San Patrignano community in Italy or the Magpie Project in the UK) and donates a hefty percentage of her profits to them, once her clothes are sold. Bethany is kind, and this attitude is a fundamental part of how her brand is perceived.

There is a total absence of kindness in the luxury-fashion sector; the entire system is built on exclusivity, and for this reason Bethany's designs, and the system she has put in place, are pioneering another way to think. Her clothes may be as expensive as a luxury label's, but her concept of giving back is the antithesis of what luxury is today.

Bethany's accolades are impressive: she was shortlisted for the LVMH Prize in 2019, and only a few months later went on to win Emerging Menswear Designer at the British Fashion Awards. Interestingly – and as a sign of the changing times – only a few years ago she wouldn't even have been considered, or taken seriously in her creative endeavours, as she would have been seen as 'too small' and 'unscaleable', which you may also read as 'irrelevant'.

Size really does matter, and in the age of the Anthropocene we need to stop believing that bigger is better, because we might be about to prove that the opposite is true: that small, manageable and responsible are more than enough. Looking once again at Mother Nature, we learn that successful systems aren't upscaled to take over, but are replicated to maximize their beneficial effect – the key word being 'abundance', not 'growth'.

Waste in fashion can be redesigned and pre-designed, and what is now a massive problem could actually become a valuable resource. As long as there are clothes being made, there will be fabric offcuts; and as long as we are wearing clothes, we will leave behind a trail of our unwanted pieces. What we need now is increased investment in creative as well as technological design solutions, in waste-cutting skills and techniques, in systemic recycling innovations in clothing production and disposal.

HOW CAN WE UPCYCLE?

Some materials, and some clothes, lend themselves to upcycling better than others. As you saw in Chapter 6, denim reigns supreme and can be cut, transformed and reassembled into almost anything. When it comes to upcycling at home, certain items, such as men's shirts, can be reused in simple ways or pretty sophisticated ones, depending on your ability to make, or if you have access to makers.

New nightwear

My favourite way to extend the life of my husband's old worn shirts is so simple: I reuse them as nightwear. More often than not, it will be the collars and cuffs that disintegrate first – so I cut them off, and that's about it. Hello to my new cotton nightie!

And speaking of nightwear, last week I did something quite unthinkable: I own a DKNY black long-sleeved cotton-and-viscose jersey dress, beautiful quality, really soft and comfortable, but which I hardly ever wore (too warm for summer, not warm enough for winter). It suddenly hit me that it would be blissful to sleep in it, so I cut off the sleeves and *voilà*: snooze-city. (What of the sleeves? I cut them up, to make wipers for my spectacles.)

Old shirts

I am also partial to making a skirt out of two old shirts – no sewing needed at all; just button one shirt up to the other, tie the sleeves around your waist and there you have it: 2 shirts = 1 skirt!

If you are good at sewing, or you know someone who is, there are several ways that shirts can live for ever.

You can make cushion covers with them, or the cutest patchwork baby duvet covers. When I had my brand, we used to make our garment bags with them, to avoid using plastic.

Old T-shirts

T-shirts are also perfect for simple, creative at-home upcycling, and often all you need is a pair of scissors, a needle and thread: you can cut the T-shirts up, turn them into vests and crop-tops, add elastic or ribbon to play with the shape or lengthen them by roughly sewing two, or three, together.

When it comes to simple, accessible and effective at-home upcycling, YouTube and the blogosphere are your best friends. All it takes is one Google search – 'how to customize a T-shirt' or 'five ways to refashion a shirt' – and you'll soon be sucked into the endless ways that you can transform your clothes at home.

KEEPING
INSTEAD

As a self-confessed clothes keeper, I am no fan of decluttering. And I am by no means precise in the way I keep my clothes; in fact I am messy, chaotic and quite untidy. Trust me, maintenance is not only for the tidy and the organized; it can fit anyone's life-style, provided you find a way that works for you.

I tend to completely rearrange my clothes once a year, but no more than that. Mostly in late spring, before the moths take over and when I become eager to re-explore my old/new-again sum-mer outfits. Inevitably, when I rearrange my clothes, I see some that have been left unworn for too long, but that I am still at-tached to, so I fold them away in a big bag and hide them in the attic (when I didn't have an attic, I kept them under my bed in a pretty vintage suitcase). I dig them out every few years, and the feeling is the same as being contacted by an old, much-loved friend after a while of not having spoken. This year I rediscov-ered an incredible midi Shantung-silk skirt (why did I ever hide it in the first place?) and I have been wearing it absolutely every-where. Have you got storage? If so, I couldn't recommend this method more – it works for me every time. You could even add your own styling to it: how about you hide away a whole look, like a time-capsule? In ten years from now, when the generations that follow will be ready to revive it, you'll have an original item.

A NEW
MINDSET

To change the system, we must change the culture it thrives on, and rethinking the role of our existing clothes and objects could be the way to move from a culture of excess to one of abundance instead. In an age of dwindling resources, every way of reusing pre-existing materials makes economic as well as environmental sense.

By now you know that, just as we are producing too many clothes, we are producing too much clothing waste, and unless we act swiftly and radically, we're stuffed. You know that you shouldn't buy something unless you love it or need it, and that if you love it, you should be prepared to mend it; and if you don't, you should find a responsible way to give it away. You know that brands have cottoned on to the crisis and something must be done to avert it, and that technology will – hopefully and eventually – save us. You know there is no time to waste.

Trash can be prevented from the onset, if we think differently in the first place. After all, the most sustainable garment is the one you already own.

Chapter 8

Tech Before
You Buy

I have said it in this book already: as we mend our broken clothes, we also need to repair the broken systems that made them. And when it comes to the systems that govern our consumption, we – the citizens, the brands' customers – have immense power of persuasion, because brands are incredibly interested in the way we shop from them.

If mending clothes is a revolutionary act, then understanding how the fashion industry works, why its operating system is broken and how to involve yourself in agitating for its betterment is a mature act of responsible citizenship. It's what we can all do to change our status quo, and to take full responsibility for our purchasing choices.

We have seen extensively (in Chapter 5) how understanding the properties of our clothing's materials can influence the way we care for them. Well, that same knowledge is even more useful to help us determine how we choose to buy. Because being attentive to what we own, and mending our clothing to maximize its longevity and diminish its environmental impact by caring for it better, has an important part to play; but awareness of fabric composition, workers' conditions and the side-effects of accelerated disposal has the potential to actually change the way we shop, which is just as important and ultimately will inform the whole process of owning responsibly.

Fortunately for us, the concept of voting with our wallets is a well-established practice, and modern technology is facilitating the process of choice-making in radical new ways: sure, it foments rampant consumerism, as the act of buying has never been so easy, but it can also invite us to try alternatives, buy differently and exercise our desire to be conscious consumers.

I always say that 'conscious' is the opposite of 'catatonic' and implies action over inaction: with the help of new technologies at our disposal, we can practise these activations more readily than ever before.

Culturally and historically, there has always been a strong link between clothes and technologies, because textiles have always been at the forefront of innovation: the invention and subsequent ingenious development of the loom, or the ability to identify the naturally-occurring chemical compounds needed to fix dyes, are statements of an industry that has always been forward-thinking. As we have seen when we looked at cotton, the Industrial Revolution owes its start to the textile-manufacturing sector.

Textiles are so inextricably linked with tech that we can consider Jacquard (a system of punch-hole cards that were used with power looms, to simplify the process of making multi-layered textiles such as brocade) as being a precursor to computing. In fact Google has recently announced that its first digital platform for smart clothing will share that name.

So it seems that this marriage is alive and kicking right now, enjoying a blissful honeymoon – there are few industries that have benefited from recent technological advancements, such as online shopping and social media, more than the fashion industry. This fact is omnipresent in our cultural landscape: cheap clothing and mass-produced luxury products are no longer simply available; they are in our faces every second, wherever we look/scroll. We have been saturated, and more and more people are beginning to respond.

The role of technology in redefining how we consume is of critical importance if we learn how to use innovation to reconnect us to our values, rather than alienate us from them.

RENTING AND RESELLING

'It's rented . . . Like Netflix for purses.'

Jennifer Hudson, *Sex and the City* movie, 2008

Let's consider fashion consumption in its most basic sense, as the buying, wearing and discarding of clothes. This is the over-arching template of consumption that we know best. But, slowly, it's changing. The rise of the secondary market and the sharing economy are only in their infancy in a fashion context, and the new modes of consumption aren't for everyone, but their ability to change fashion lies in our ability to selectively engage with the ones that suit our lifestyles.

Clothing rental may be a late entry into the sharing-economy game, but it is growing in popularity on a global scale: from Rent the Runway in the USA all the way to Y Closet in China, the concept is spreading rapidly. It was preceded by car-sharing apps, house-sharing apps (hello, Airbnb) and, of course, the now-obsolete pioneer: the video-rental powerhouse that was Blockbuster (RIP).

The success of renting is partly due to the fact that it relies on the largely female tradition of sharing clothes among peers, repackaged from the basic asking your mate next door, 'Can I borrow your designer piece for this wedding I am going to? I promise I will have it dry-cleaned afterwards and give it back as good as new', into the now-familiar scenario of download app, Like, press Confirm, and wait for delivery.

Personally, I am still unconvinced that renting represents clean innovation, from an environmental standpoint, because I am concerned that an upscaled rental system includes an enormous amount of transport and dry cleaning (it also includes a fair bit of 'buying', because rental companies need to purchase the goods they will rent, much as a retailer does, as clients will still want to rent the latest seasonal trends). However, I am convinced that it is changing the way we perceive ownership, and to me that element is what makes it an interesting phenomenon.

Because the interest in renting, and the rise of the secondary market (which is growing ten times faster than mainstream fashion and is predicted by many to overtake fast fashion in the near future), coincides with the rise of a generation for whom clothes represent no emotional attachment whatsoever, disposability is the name of the game.

However, kids are no longer just throwing away; they are increasingly reselling their barely worn clothes on Depop, eBay, thredUP and Thrift+, implementing an innate cycle of reuse and rewear, which follows from the fact that they consider it really uncool to be wearing (and sharing) their clothes more than once or twice. Encouragingly, as well as selling their old clothes, they are also buying other people's pre-loved garments with the same enthusiasm, and then selling them on after a few frivolous wears.

Clothes have lost their allure, making it easier to inhabit them for a short while before getting rid of them, which is why the rise in rentals, like teenagers trading their used clothing, is largely due to a lack of attachment towards our possessions, rather than the environmental necessity to improve our consumption habits. This isn't necessarily a bad thing – sometimes things that occur spontaneously are longer-lasting than things that are prescribed.

Speaking with my teenage daughter always gives me an advantage and insight into what is actually happening: her state-school education in South London provides me with a balanced view of her teenage peers' hopes and habits. She too has noticed a marked increase in her friends becoming concerned with the environmental crisis, since the recent climate strikes and Fridays For Future protests, driven by young people demanding a future.

Many concerned students are responding by changing their diets, with increasing numbers choosing to become vegans; but most of them do not – yet – make the connection that fashion, like food, has a direct impact both on people and planet, just as meat and dairy do. They do not know that our skin is the second most-absorbing organ after our stomach, and that pesticides that are dangerous in food are just as dangerous in the clothes we wear.

Potentially the lack of credible involvement from their modern-day heroes – Instagrammers, pop stars and YouTubers – shows a lack of peer-to-peer pressure when it comes to seeing clothes as a vehicle for catalysing change: all too often, influencers will take up a charitable cause, only to abandon its principles by the time the next post is due, which, for a generation obsessed with authenticity, leads to conflicting messages that are harder to uptake.

It strikes me that clothing is always second-tier when we commit to behaviour change. We know that we need to eat less meat, take fewer flights, drive less – but fashion feels less understood as a driver of climate heating.

TIY

Technology is facilitating transactions and opening up previously unimagined opportunities to globalize the secondary market, and it really looks like a whole new fashion horizon. While until recently, sharing, repairing and buying second-hand was a circumspect affair, we now see innovative online initiatives replicating all over – apps and platforms to buy vintage and pre-loved, to swap, to connect you to your closest mending facilities and to help you maximize your wardrobe's use and minimize unnecessary buying. You can do it all at the press of an icon, and it is super-easy both ways: both buying and selling.

This is, of course, absolutely brilliant, and a real transformative step for this industry. However, we mustn't think that the rise of the secondary market alone will alleviate the problem, because in itself it won't, not unless it comes with a whole change to the system. Reselling something you've worn for a minute to make space to keep buying new is not a solution; keeping and maintaining for as long as possible is still, and by far, the best option that we have for slowing down mass production. If we buy less, brands will be forced to produce less – it is as simple as that.

The best place to start is your own wardrobe. Just as you

might experiment with styling your outfits differently, why don't you actually analyse what's in there and consider the best course of action to make your clothes be of use – to you or others – for the longest time?

You could start by measuring your clothing carbon footprint (there's an app for that) and see how well you are doing; and you can continue by checking how transparent your favourite brands actually are (there's an app for that, too). Then you could look at your clothes and start to categorize them (yes, there's an app for that as well). Find those apps and try them. I promise you, there are some really brilliant ones around.

Experiment with your clothes – do something new. Renew them, refresh them, give them a chance, give them away, but remember that they are permanent, their materials are permanent and we are never really getting rid of anything we throw; we're simply letting it clog the planet rather than our wardrobe. The more we feed on used clothing, the less we need to buy new ones; and the fewer clothes we buy, the more likely we are to buy responsibly, accurately and with full awareness, instead of on a whim.

CLOTHING CYCLES
FOR LIFETIME USE

My cousins and I have been sharing clothes, and keeping many of them in a seemingly endless circulation cycle, for the best part of half a century. I come from a generation when passing clothes on was not restricted to families of low income, but was in fact practised by most people, except those who had more money than sense.

The rules were quite basic, and clear: while you were growing up, clothes weren't really 'yours', but were programmed to be worn until they no longer fitted, to be passed on subsequently to the second in line, and then to the third, fourth, fifth, and so on. In my close-knit family I was the last sibling after two brothers, but the fourth in line to inherit my female cousins' clothes. We all wore the same smock dresses, the same shoes, the same communion gown, even the same pyjamas.

As adults, my cousins and I still pass things round on a regular basis, and I would say that a good quarter of my wardrobe (and bits of my daughters' wardrobes, too) contains clothes from this cycle of life. In many instances we don't even remember who they originated with; we just know we've all worn them at some point, and we remember the stories each of us lived while wearing them.

This rich culture of familial recycling is almost lost for ever, overtaken by memory-less clothes – clothes that are all the same and don't merit this kind of love and attention. I still buy all my clothes with my cousins in mind, as well as several other people, whom I know will eventually love them after I have loved them.

You could now, with the use of technology, construct this kind of system between you and your friends, family and extended community: where everyone knows what everyone else has in their wardrobes, and everyone can interact within them.

RETURN
TO LANDFILL

Of course, wherever technology can improve standards of living and solve problems, it holds the parallel possibility of causing destruction, and this can only increase if the future of the industry, and technology's role within it, is still hell-bent on exponential growth, more products, more sales, easier and faster buying.

Let's look at online returns, for instance. In the past (or BOS – Before Online Shopping) you could safely take something you had bought but not worn back to your local boutique (or wherever else you had physically made the purchase), and that item would be reabsorbed into the rails – no questions asked – provided there was no damage or sign of evident usage. You'd have to take it back, in person, and show your receipt to a human being, but overall a quick steam and a tag change would be all that was needed to ensure the garment was back in circulation in next to no time.

In this current age of the Anthropocene, and for the sake of Queen Convenience, returning – much like buying – is done blindly, impersonally, especially when buying from huge online retailers.

Yes, online has made returning even easier. Yes, all you have to do is shove said item back in a plastic bag (which it comes in, just in case). Yes, you can actually wear it and still send it back. Yes, you can order four sizes and decide, after trying them all on, which one is the better fit and return the rest. Yes, out of sight, out of mind.

A 2018 survey actually found that around one in ten Brits admits to buying clothes online, posting images of them on social media and then returning the items for a full refund.

Forgive me for spinning a new ending, but this Father Christmas myth that we can simply return items at will is bullshit: returns these days are a massive problem because, in the majority of cases, returns are not resold. Shockingly, most online purchases that are returned end up as rubbish.

The reason is simple: giant online retailers, operating from giant warehouses, lack the capacity to check and reintroduce returns into the main system, so they are stored separately and not, so to speak, put back on the shopping rails: it's not financially effective to pay someone to unpack these returned goods, examine them for flaws or fix them, if they appear, repackage them and update inventory numbers.

As returns languish in no-man's land, time passes, fashion's unique planned obsolescence by design means they go out of season pretty damn fast, and they are then either sold at a discounted price to third-party liquidators and resellers, who transport them hundreds of miles away (often in half-full trucks, adding unnecessary negative impact to an already OTT environmental burden), or destroyed either by landfill or incineration, as that is always the quickest way to get rid of valueless excess. While many retailers will admit to actively throwing away at least 25 per cent of their returns, they often lack the full view to account for the rest, so nobody truly knows what's going on.

In this case, technology is not helping, but is exacerbating a problem, by creating an unaccounted, un-transparent maze where our returns, quite simply, get lost. A mega-glitch in a seemingly efficient system.

If the fashion system was truly based on efficiency and quality, returns would have value and would be seen as a further monetizable resource. There should be a system within the system to return them to the shop floor, rather than returning them straight into landfill. People should be employed to intervene, repair and re-upload regularly, and from the inside.

At present there are a few, solitary examples of companies that provide repairs and alterations on behalf of fashion brands. Trove, whose mission statement is 'We work with those who see the value of resale – and are ready for it', recuperates consumer seconds for Patagonia, Eileen Fisher and a handful of illuminated labels (in denim in particular) that provide in-house mending and aftercare; but it's by no means endemic. If fashion brands were to understand the true value of their offerings, surely they would endeavour to exploit them to the fullest.

Of course, it is challenging to integrate something so slow and individualistic as mending within a structure as gigantic and fast as the global fashion industry – it won't be easy to capture excess and surplus before it is disposed of, and then reintroduce it as something of value into the system that rejected it. It is like swimming against the tide.

I can see mending facilities located close to immense warehouses dedicated to customizing returned stock; I see people with new job descriptions like 'creative waste engineer', 'returns re-uploader' or 'reclaiming manager', allocated within brands and factories to redivert excesses and surplus; I see opportunities to train people in learning new skills; I see small and big living next to each other and different rhythms cohabiting in harmony.

But above all I see beautiful, unique products saved from destruction and reclaimed to live. I also see something that I see every day, but hardly ever notice: I see nature among the skyscrapers, a computer sitting next to a bowl of ripe fruit, my cat asleep on the bonnet of my car. This is how we humans live: among the things we inherited from nature and the things we made ourselves. We can't have one without the other.

CULTURAL APPROPRIATION *vs* CULTURAL APPRECIATION

As with the burden associated with over-consumption (such as returns), availability and visibility leading to easy access carry their own complications. We have seen in Chapter 3 how the wonderful world of the Web is facilitating and invigorating making and learning new and old crafting techniques, and we know that the rapid spread of 'direct to consumer' platforms is increasing visibility, and trade, for communities of artisans all over the world.

However, the flipside of the rise in increased visibility is that it has become increasingly easy to copy, misuse and disrespect other cultures – borrowing their traditions for a commercial gain from which they won't benefit – and increasingly difficult for citizens to understand the difference between appreciation and appropriation.

'The term "Cultural Appropriation" may be overused, but only because the negative power dynamic that is used to describe it is all too common. It is about power, and always exists within a framework of oppression and colonialism. It exists within the double-edged sword of cultural erasure and cultural theft. It's not just the theft, it's the hypocrisy. It's not about "culture policing" or "you can't say anything any more" as conservative rhetoric would have it. Yet even in the most blatant cases we must use the opportunity for conversation rather than simple finger-pointing.'

Céline Semaan, founder of the Slow Factory

Fortunately, the Internet and social media are increasing scrutiny and somehow facilitating industry watchdogs. One example is the Instagram account 'Diet Prada', launched in 2014 by two fashion-industry co-workers with a great sense of humour. The account, which at the time of writing has grown to more than 1.8 million followers, began by drawing the blatant comparison between one designer's catwalk show and another's, to highlight and ridicule the end of originality in fashion, and to ask us all to take the industry a little less seriously. But as the catwalks have copied and assaulted cultures the world over, the account has stepped up to highlight their behaviour to a community that holds designers and brands accountable.

It is one thing to buy a piece directly from the community that made it, and who will prosper from your custom – it is quite another to buy a designer copy of that piece, without checking if the people who inspired it are actually benefiting from its profits. When it comes to cultural appreciation and its nemesis, *cultural appropriation*, the line that divides them is fragile, like a badly sewn hem with a disintegrating thread.

In her book *Who Owns Culture*, the lawyer, legal scholar and author Susan Scafidi defines cultural appropriation as 'Taking intellectual property, traditional knowledge, cultural expressions, or artifacts from someone else's culture without permission'. It sounds simple enough, and is an all-too-recognizable feat in an age of mass-produced 'Turkish' rugs available from IKEA and 'Aztec'-print everything gracing Urban Outfitters. Yet applying Scafidi's definition in the context of everyday design choices is a complicated endeavour.

In the process of obtaining permission, does one need to seek permission from every member of the given culture, or is it sufficient to seek out an authority figure? Scafidi's '3 S Test' was created to help designers and business people alike avoid the misappropriation of culture. It goes as follows:

> ☞ **Source**: Has the source been involved in the production and creation of the item? Has the source given you permission? For example, if a brand is selling a Turkish rug, has it been made in Turkey, or in Honduras?
>
> ☞ **Similarity**: How similar is the item to that which inspires it? For example, is the item vaguely reminiscent of its inspiration source or is it a complete copy?
>
> ☞ **Significance**: How significant is the item or design to the culture? For example, is it sacred, is it part of a religious ceremony, and so on?

Scafidi's book, *Who Owns Culture*, was published more than 15 years ago, and yet our tendency towards cultural theft has hardly waned. Yet again we are faced with the fact that our limited understanding has fuelled our conveniences; that we'd rather buy that cute little top with a Mexican-inspired print all over it without bothering to question whether those symbols are private, or religious, or even if they are correctly represented.

Some of you might think that this is petty, even slightly OTT, until you turn the table and regard it from a selfish point of view: imagine *your* family photo album (or secret recipe) being 'borrowed' by a corporation, mass-produced, packaged and sold for a profit, without your explicit consent and without you having received a share of those profits. Take it one step further: imagine if the ancestors of the corporation in question had actually killed, maimed and humiliated your own ancestors before obtaining the photos, and are now using your family history to enrich their own identity, beaming with pride and making tons of money in the process, while you get nothing.

In the future – and the future starts now – we should all make ourselves responsible to ensure this doesn't happen any more, and demand that whoever wishes to use something that doesn't belong to them asks first, and shares all revenues equally.

Carry Somers, Fashion Revolution's co-founder, is an outspoken voice when it comes to this topic. Her multi-award-winning fair-trade brand Pachacuti has been working with indigenous panama-hat weavers in Ecuador since the late 1980s.

She writes:

> Explanations of cultural appropriation arguments too often revolve solely around power, and the imbalances of that power. The normal argument goes that it is dominant/colonial/white/western/capitalist exploitation of a less privileged/subjugated/minority/dispossessed/voiceless culture. Whilst power is important, it isn't all about power and this narrative needs to be rewritten. Cultural borrowing can be positive, not just problematic, and fashion, as well as music, art and other cultural expressions would be far poorer without it . . .
> To carry this conversation forward, we need to imagine new ways to credit the source of 'inspiration' and integrate this into design practice, as well as drawing up new legislative frameworks to better protect communities. A new law is passing through the Mexican legislature on Safeguarding the Knowledge, Culture and Identity of Indigenous and Afro-Mexican Peoples and Communities. The new law will recognize collective ownership rights over their cultural expressions and sanction third parties who use, market or exploit elements of their culture or identity without the corresponding consent. The hope is that this will create a blueprint for other countries to

follow. In the meantime, until the culture of the industry changes and until legislation comes into force to protect communities, all of us as global citizens can make more responsible fashion choices and support brands who work directly with these communities, giving them the respect and remuneration that they deserve.

It is, as always, about finding a balance, which is the hardest of all tasks. As with the #MeToo movement, where does the terrifying reality of sexual abuse and inappropriate behaviour start and the less consequential 'sexy banter' stop? And shouldn't we put a firm stop to that banter, now that we know that the culture accepting of it also fosters the abuse that follows it? Because when a habit is 'less bad' than horrendous, it still should be nipped in the bud. So although I am not suggesting that you should bring your lawyer each time you shop for something artisanal or ethnic, I am encouraging everyone to take this complicated subject seriously, even if it does mean googling terminologies that are unfamiliar, or revising your understanding of history.

Being creative with your clothes is not only about how you construct your look; it's also about constructing your beliefs. Being elegant and smart is not only about cut and silhouette; it's also about being brave enough to experiment with new mindsets, having the courage to try new things and the confidence to trust they are right for you.

And you don't have to be into fashion to try – you could just as well be into human rights, or environmentalism, because this isn't solely about the way we look, but is also about the way we dress: monotonous or exhilarating, acquiring clothes is something we all have to do and, once we acquire them, we are responsible for them. Understanding where their raw materials originate from, knowing where they were made, by whom and in what conditions, caring for them in order to maximize their longevity, and having an afterlife strategy for when they become obsolete to you may seem laborious, but it is necessary.

You have done this before, in other areas of your life, I am sure. You've questioned the food you eat at some point, and acted accordingly, whether it lasted or not; you've been angered by something badly enough to withdraw your custom, permanently or temporarily (and you probably also tweeted your resentment and took the time to google to see if others felt the same); you check the ingredients, you compare prices, you read the reviews. Do the same with your clothes. Make informed decisions and take up responsible ways to interact with the system that you wish to see made better. We lead by example – we make the trends.

Check this one out: buying responsibly is in; buying new is old; buying used is cool – and keeping is the ultimate reward.

Chapter 9

Transparency
Is Trending

By now you should be in no doubt that the fashion system is broken at its core, with multiple tears appearing like the unstoppable moth holes in a woollen jumper. These holes, left unattended, are becoming larger and increasingly hard to mend; some holes are roughly patched – a temporary job done to avoid further damage – but in the majority of cases, despite the fact that we can imagine that some damage has occurred, it is kept deliberately hidden from our eyesight in a state of unrepair and degradation.

To repair something broken you need to inspect it first (*what kind of damage has been done?*); diagnose it and stabilize it (*checking the breakage and preventing further damage before it can be repaired*); decide upon the right tools and techniques for the job (*wool thread or cotton? large or thin needle? darning or patch?*); and proceed with patience and vision (*it will take time, but stitch upon stitch you will work over the damage, connect the broken threads and resolve the issue*).

Mending fashion and mending a jumper follow a similar, metaphorical trajectory, and when applying due diligence to a fashion supply chain we could be asking very similar questions:

- ☞ **Where is the damage?**: Locate it within the supply chain. Is it at the manufacturing stage or before that?
- ☞ **Diagnose it and stabilize it**: Is it social or environmental? What set of actions will it take?
- ☞ **Find the right tools**: Is it legislation or innovation that will improve the problem?
- ☞ **Proceed with patience and vision**: It will take time, but policy upon policy, brands, governments and organizations will work over the damage and resolve the issue.

Caring for our clothes isn't separate from fashion's human-rights impact – the two are completely intertwined. Because if we really value the people who make our clothes, we will want to respect their labour and toil, their skills and handiwork, their working environment, and ensure that our buying guarantees a dignified life to all supply-chain workers.

PRICE OVER PROVENANCE

It is an innate part of our human nature to want to know where things come from. Throughout history, and especially while industrialization was more localized, orally transmitted information about our clothes, food and everyday items was readily available. In fact, until a few short generations ago, when buying a new garment it would not have been uncommon to know the provenance of the cloth; and there was often little doubt as to who made it, simply because the industry itself was much closer to home and, more importantly, because the source and make of a garment determined the quality and prestige, making it also a matter of importance in terms of your social standing to know the origins of your clothes.

We also had a better understanding of the geography of the textile industry back then, and we instinctively used that map to add or detract value from a piece of cloth at first sight. The softest woollens came from Italy; and the purest silk was Chinese or Indian; cashmere was sheared and spun in Mongolia; and the crispiest linen was grown in France. Classic tailoring was exclusively British; its Italian counterpart may have boasted equally beautiful stitching and construction, but that pesky habit the Italians had of innovating on shape and cut according to current trends made it look like an upstart. I clearly remember being in London in the 1970s and finding it outrageously funny that men in suits still wore skinny trousers straight from the 1950s, while menswear tailoring in Italy had already given way to the flared trouser in line with more contemporary styles.

As for the USA, that was known for casual wear: sneakers, denim and T-shirts; why would you buy a pair of jeans or Converse sneakers that *weren't* made in the USA? They wouldn't have been 'real', or 'original', if they had been made anywhere else, just as you wouldn't buy a tartan skirt in Hawaii or a pair of lederhosen in Harrods.

The whole character of the clothes we bought depended on the materials they were made from and the place they were sewn in, with regions being a reliable measure and assurance of quality, style and authenticity. Of course, this shift away from product literacy didn't happen in a vacuum. It coincided with the rise of offshore production and the birth of 'the Brand'. In her 1999 book *No Logo* Naomi Klein quotes Nike CEO Phil Knight's admission:

'For years we thought of ourselves as a production-oriented company, meaning we put all our emphasis on designing and manufacturing the product. But now we understand that the most important thing we do is market the product. We've come around to saying that Nike is a marketing-oriented company, and the product is our most important marketing tool.'

It was this concept that moved us from the age of provenance to the age of brand identity. Rather than focus on quality and manufacturing, brands came to focus on the intrinsic values they were selling with the product, rather than the product itself. You now buy Nike sneakers to look cool, and a Gillette razor to be a real man. This separation of people from product is a driving force behind the widespread nonchalance towards the fashion industry's human-rights abuses. We can more easily turn a blind eye to the human cost of our stuff because we don't really understand the labour it requires. Bronwyn Seier, content manager at Fashion Revolution and a graduate of the prestigious Fashion Futures MA at the London College of Fashion, wrote in *Sophomore* magazine:

> *'I was in high school when Forever 21 opened their first store in my home city. I remember buying 5 or 6 things for less than a hundred bucks with a feeling of disbelief on opening day. I also remember telling myself it was probably all so cheap because it was made by robots, or something. Since those days, I've learned that fashion remains the most human labour intensive manufacturing industry, due to the fact that robots don't know what to do with soft materials in the way they know how to assemble Hondas or iPhones. Having stitched an impressive number of lapel collars, fly fronts, and patch pockets during my stint as a fashion student, I can no longer shirk the question of fast fashion's true cost. I know how much time it takes to construct a collar or line a jacket.'*

I have written about care-labels telling stories that are incomplete, stopping the narrative halfway through the 'once upon a time' and the 'happily ever after'. And when it comes to the real provenance of our clothes, the origins of the raw materials they were fabricated from, and the many processes that are undertaken to produce them, labels are an even less reliable source of information.

Essentially, in a deregulated industry such as fashion, there are no legal obligations when it comes to listing ingredients, provenance, working practices and sell-by dates, making it truly impossible to understand the full picture. We may know that a garment was made with polyester, and sewn (at least partly) in Malaysia, but we will not be able, with that information alone, to locate the exact place that polyester was extracted from or processed; nor can we guarantee that the 'made in . . .' information provides the whole story, as garments could be cut in a facility, but assembled and sewn somewhere else entirely.

This lack of transparency, and the subsequent inability to trace the provenance of a garment and its raw materials, make for all sorts of murky waters in between.

'Transparency by itself will not solve the industry's problems, but it provides an important window into the conditions in which our clothes are being made. What we each do with the information being disclosed by big brands and retailers is most important of all. It is with access to information that we hold brands and retailers, governments and suppliers to account. We see transparency as the first step towards wider systemic change for a safer, fairer and cleaner global fashion industry.'

Sarah Ditty, Fashion Revolution policy director

WHY TRANSPARENCY?

The fashion panorama has changed dramatically and at increasing speed over the past 40 years, and has become unrecognizable from the more localized system that was in place before globalization. As we have seen in Chapter 2, before the move to China and other largely unregulated shores, many fashion brands owned their own mills and manufacturer, or relied on their local infrastructure. However, as sewing skills and capabilities in Chinese-operated factories grew, it didn't take long for fashion to cotton on to the huge potential that an exploited, non-unionized workforce and zero environmental protection would have on things such as margins and profits.

The present fashion industry is built on secrecy, its supply chain disconnected at every stage of the manufacturing process, with brands and their producers often operating alone and fragmented – caught up in an arrangement where invisibility defines the rules, leading to gross inefficiency, opaqueness and a system where human-rights violations and environmental abuses are hidden, and justified.

In fact the way the supply chain works is a perfect mirror of the culture that this industry thrives on: closed doors, elitism, imbalances of power, and exclusion of practically everyone bar the anointed few. These attributes are manifest throughout, from the way fashion portrays itself in advertising and social media, to the way it treats its workers, from garment makers to student interns.

The fashion industry seconds exploitation and abusive behaviour; it has them embedded as part of its image, and power reigns supreme in even the smallest of hierarchies. Treating others as you wouldn't wish to be treated yourself is tantamount to a daily pastime, which is precisely why transparency is one of the most disruptive agents when it comes to moving forward, because it challenges just about everything this industry stands for.

Transparency brings visibility and accountability, and right now we need a fashion industry that better understands its own inner workings and respects the people who work in its value chain. What we need is a clear, uninterrupted line of vision from the product's origin to its disposal, to foster dignity, empowerment and justice for the people who make our clothes, and to protect the environment we all share.

Although we can't undo the way our existing clothes were made, we should nevertheless be aware of their social impact and consider how little – or how much – we really know. Take your eyes off this book for a few seconds and think: *What am I wearing?* Rather like with mindful meditation (but instead of focusing on your inner self), take a look at your second skin – the clothes you are wearing – and ask yourself a few questions.

THE LOVE CHECK

☐ What am I wearing right now?

☐ Do I remember where I bought it?

☐ Do I know who made it?

☐ Do I know where it was made?

☐ Did I check the label for this info before I bought it?

☐ Do I love it enough to mend it or have it repaired if it breaks?

☐ Have I, in fact, ever checked the labels inside?

☐ Do I have any plans for it at end-of-life?

The exploitation that is so prevalent in the fashion supply chain today is made even more humiliating under the lens of disposability. If a piece has been made under conditions of forced labour, or illegal low pay, that is a tragedy in itself. But the fact that the garment made will also enter a cycle of disrespect, bought to be thrown away after two wears, begs the question 'why?' Why exploit people in the pursuit of producing rubbish?

A while back, accepting the *Elle* Style Awards 'Conscious Award' in 2017, I said something that has now been quoted time and time again: 'It isn't enough just looking for quality in the products we buy, we must insist that there is quality in the lives of the people who make them.'

MAPPING AND PUBLISHING/ SUPPLY-CHAIN TIERS 1, 2 AND 3

In practical terms, transparency is only the first step towards a responsible industry, because transparency is, in itself, no guarantee of best practice – it is merely a form of mapping after all, and in many cases it raises more questions than it answers – but it does provide us with comparable information and, above all, it forces brands to become accountable for their actions. Crucially, it also facilitates the work of unions, NGOs and human-rights organizations on the ground, as well as encouraging citizens to be vigilant, to keep asking questions and to verify whether they actually trust the answers they are given.

As the fashion industry touches many other industries, starting with agriculture all the way to communication, its value chain is not vertical, or easy to locate. Add to this the global routes that have come to define fashion manufacturing and you'll see that any kind of accurate mapping is both complicated and expensive to put into place.

Simply speaking, the supply chain is divided into three 'tiers': the first one, and the easiest to locate and map, is where the products are manufactured, but it may also include labelling and packaging. The second tier is for mills and wet processing, where fabrics are woven and/or dyed. The third tier is for raw materials, where cotton or sheep are farmed, or the forest where the viscose is pulped from.

FINISHED PRODUCT	TIER 1	TIER 2	TIER 3
For example, a shirt	**CUT, MAKE, TRIM**	**MILLS AND WET PROCESSING**	**RAW MATERIALS**
	Where the products are cut out and sewn together, labelled and packaged	Where yarns are woven or knitted into cloth, and the fabric is dyed and finished	Where sheep are farmed for wool, or cotton is grown, or trees are grown for viscose, etc.

Brands rarely own their own manufacturing facilities any more; they contract their goods instead, and this new system has in turn fostered the rise of middlemen, creating a dense fog in between brands and suppliers. In that fog, all sorts of things can and do happen – from child labour to illegal waste-dumping – and all sorts of things get lost too, like the guarantee that products are made where they say they are.

Unauthorized subcontracting happens when a factory is over-burdened with orders and passes some on to another factory, without alerting their client (the brand). Or it can happen because a brand has brought down the price of a product so low that the factory owner decides it can only pass it on to a cheaper factory, again without letting the brand know.

Once again I return to Naomi Klein's investigation on the rise of brand identity. In the 1990s, as companies invested in the mythology of their brand, they abandoned responsibility for their products. In Chapter 9 of Klein's book *No Logo*, Walter Landor, branding-agency president, tells the author, 'Products are made in the factory, but brands are made in the mind.' But companies didn't simply figuratively abandon the product; they disowned their factories altogether. Klein writes, 'When the actual man-ufacturing process is so devalued, it stands to reason that the people doing the work of production are likely to be treated like detritus – the stuff left behind.'

Clothing companies no longer *make* clothing, they *sell* it. And this is where the need for transparency begins.

AUDITS

Audits are systems that are put into place in order to evaluate contractors' and suppliers' working practices and to ensure their quality, social, environmental and security compliance. These audits are merely a way to diagnose and, if not coupled with a list of 'recommendations', it's a bit like going to the doctor to get a diagnosis without a prescription or any kind of aftercare. Because audits are undertaken to accredit or certify a brand or manufacturer, they too often lack detail, action and remediation.

In most cases, auditing acts as an inhibitor to full transparency, providing a system that does not encourage improvement of working conditions, and at best is just a diagnostic tool, but certainly not a cure. Not only have audit systems on many occasions proved to be faulty, but they are widely seen as a strategic pact between retailers and producers to delegate responsibilities to third parties – in this case the auditing companies, which are not even legally accountable anyway.

Of all labour accreditation standards, the most respected and commonly used to certify organizations' demonstrated commitment to the fair treatment of workers is the SA8000 (Social Accountability International). For environmental impact there are several angles to look at, so these are some of the main bodies that provide specific certifications: Global Organic Textile Standard (GOTS), Global Recycle Standard and Oeko-Tex Standard 100.

The only auditing that has a meaningful impact nowadays is one that works towards establishing the correct application of those recognized worldwide standards. There are lists provided by organizations such as CO (Common Objective) available online.

In short, an audit will capture a moment in time, a 'day in the life' of a producing factory, with no real guarantee that good practices are followed through consistently in the rest of the year, meaning that regular audits – and preferably audits that are unannounced – are the only way to keep a thorough check. Unfortunately, suppliers are often alerted that an audit will take place, which gives them ample time to prepare and hide bad practice, as was exposed in the case of refugee children illegally working in Turkey being, quite literally, hidden in adjacent rooms or asked to temporarily vacate the premises to avoid being caught.

I have personal experience when it comes to this. In 2008–11 my husband and I collaborated with a leading supermarket to create what was to be the first upscaled, upcycled online collection made entirely from remnants and surplus from their facilities in Sri Lanka. While visiting the factories we were shown one of the biggest local mills and, above all, the warehouse where all the obsolete and leftover stock was kept: an enormous space housing thousands and thousands of rolls of fabrics that had previously been discarded and from which we chose our selection.

To celebrate the launch of the collection in 2010 I returned to Sri Lanka accompanied by a *Daily Telegraph* journalist who was writing a story on how the project had come to exist. I returned to the same mill and asked if I could take the journalist to see the warehouse, only to be told that it didn't exist.

Similarly, a few years later we were consulting on a major high-street-store Reclaim-to-Wear capsule collection and went to visit one of their main suppliers in the Anatolia region, to pre-design the line. The owner of the factory had been alerted to the fact that we were looking for surplus and waste, and promptly removed it before we arrived; and the factory, despite being in full production season, had been completely cleaned up, with all signs of any waste removed from sight. When we asked where all the offcuts were, or the excess rolls, we were told that the facility didn't produce any waste at all!

IF WE CAN'T SEE IT, WE CAN'T FIX IT

'If we can't see it, we can't fix it.' This has been one of our most important mottos since Fashion Revolution's inception. When an industry lacks transparency, bad things are allowed to happen.

The fashion-industry facade crumbled along with the Rana Plaza factory complex in Dhaka, Bangladesh, in the early morning of 24 April 2013, killing 1,138 people, mostly young women, and injuring more than 2,500.

The disaster – the worst industrial disaster in the fashion industry to date – was by no means the first, and unfortunately won't be the last either, but its severity, and the gruesome pictures that emerged and were widely shared online and in the global news, became a turning point, a moment of reckoning; and the tide has been turning, albeit slowly, ever since.

The Rana Plaza factory complex was a huge building, producing clothes for some of the best-known brands in the world, the majority of the type that we would call 'fast fashion', but also quite a few that would be considered 'premium' or even 'luxury' household names. However, due to the total lack of transparency and accountability, which was absolutely the norm at the time, it became pretty obvious very soon after the tragedy that pointing the finger at those responsible was going to take time, because it was nearly impossible to know for sure exactly which brands had been using the facility.

Behind-the-scenes stories tell of brands' CEOs and CFOs frantically calling their own sourcing departments to find out whether Rana Plaza was in fact one of their suppliers, and in many cases this information couldn't be traced, due to a web of subcontracting and chaotic sourcing practices. It took weeks to establish who was and who wasn't producing there, and the bulk of the detective work was done by activist organizations on the ground, looking for incriminating labels among the rubble.

The Clean Clothes Campaign, a global garment-worker-rights NGO, and its UK partner, Labour Behind the Label, ultimately identified 29 global brands that had recent or current orders with at least one of the five garment factories in the Rana Plaza building. The list leaves almost no Western consumer untouched (or unclothed). Yet only those very few brands that had some degree of supply-chain visibility were in a position to accept full responsibility, start a process of recovery and take immediate steps towards compensation; the majority of brands produced in the Rana Plaza complex had absolutely no idea that they had unknowingly been using the facility as a contractor.

Primark was the first brand to put their hands up, admitting that the factory had indeed been a supplier of theirs, and to offer families short-term compensation. Months after the tragedy, and following an International Labour Organization (ILO)-convened meeting where Rana Plaza-producing brands were subjected to major scrutiny, a few other brands joined in compensating the victims' families. It took a long time to get the full picture, and an even longer time to come to a decent compensation agreement, with only seven of the 29 brands that were producing onsite signing the Rana Plaza Donors Trust Fund compensation fund, which was backed by the ILO. Benetton took one year of pressure to comply, after more than one million people signed a petition calling on the brand to join the compensation fund. They paid only £740,000.

THE WORKERS

It's hard to identify and relate to the circumstances of a Bangladeshi garment worker: long hours, six-day work weeks, hot and cramped working conditions with poor air circulation, low pay, very few breaks and frequent abuses. But it's even harder to fathom being in those workers' shoes on 24 April 2013, because they were fully aware that a potential disaster was unfolding and yet they were told that production must go on.

This is the most outrageous aspect of the whole sorry affair – the fact that many garment workers had seen the cracks in the walls for days before the actual collapse, and had tried to alert their managers and supervisors. Of course, they weren't taken seriously, perhaps not even heard; and, despite an evacuation the day before the collapse, they were made to return to work the next fateful day, despite the cracks, despite the fear.

Imagine what it must have felt like to be forcibly working while simultaneously fearing for your life, not knowing whether you'd be home with your family at the end of the day; feeling the outrage of being imprisoned in a visibly crumbling building for the sake of a few million T-shirts and somebody else's profits. But those T-shirts were produced, labelled and boxed, at that time, under those circumstances, by garment workers justifiably freaking out. And those T-shirts were most likely delivered into stores – and we bought them. Those T-shirts, made in terror, in humiliation and in semi-captivity, are the reason why everything must change: all our clothing should be rigorously and accountably made with dignity. If the Rana Plaza story, as I've written it, feels far away, it shouldn't: we all own garments made in exploitation.

It's not simply the chemicals and toxicants that affect our environment and pollute the clothes we wear that are harmful to us – the lack of human dignity, the chemistry that is passed on (metaphorically as well as physically) in the act of sewing something, the conditions of those hands at work should feel just as toxic for our bodies and for our souls.

Nazma Akter, a Bangladeshi trade unionist, former garment worker and founder of the AWAJ Foundation, wrote in the 2019 edition of Fashion Revolution's *Fashion Transparency Index*:

'Transparency is needed by every major multinational fashion brand and retailer in order to help workers understand what the brands whose clothes they are making are doing to uphold workers' rights. To me, transparency also means that brands are willing to be held accountable for their business practices.

My organization uses the information disclosed by major fashion brands in various ways. For example, we share information with workers so they can negotiate for better working conditions and get their peers and managers involved too. We also use transparency information to understand good practices that brands are doing.

We would like to see more brands and retailers share information that is helpful to trade unions and garment workers such as supplier lists, audit reports and activities designed to advance freedom of association and social dialogue.'

AND FASHION
REVOLUTION WAS BORN . . .

In the few days that followed the Rana Plaza collapse, the frustration within the 'eco-fashion' community, and the downright shock experienced by those outside it, was palpable: the Tazreen factory fire (which had happened in 2012, killing 117 people and further injuring 200) was still fresh in everybody's memory, despite the fact that it had barely made a dent in public opinion.

The Rana Plaza tragedy had been predicted and could have been avoided, making it even more poignant and outrageous; and, for those of us who had been assiduously advocating better standards for the fashion supply chain, it felt like a terrifying manifestation of precisely the reasons behind our advocacy. Basically, it was the worst 'I told you so' moment that one could ever have wished for.

Fashion Revolution was born accidentally, and quite spontaneously, shortly afterwards. At the time I still had my brand, and was also working with the British Fashion Council as curator of Estethica, the sustainable fashion area at London Fashion Week, which my husband Filippo Ricci and I had co-founded in 2006.

Carry Somers, who at the time was one of our Estethica exhibitors with her panama-hat brand Pachacuti, called me after having a brainwave in the bath. She left a message on my phone asking me if I would be interested in becoming involved with her in a 'Fashion Revolution Day' to celebrate garment workers, and for this day to become an annual occurrence, on 24 April, in memory of the people who lost their lives in the Rana Plaza collapse.

I jumped at it immediately, and although I am not a strategist, I had the vision, the creativity, the experience and the contacts to try and make a start on something bigger than simply a commemorative event once a year. Our phenomenal founding team, which was hand-picked from an already well-established community that had flourished in the UK partly because of Estethica (as well as other pioneering organizations, such as Tamsin Lejeune's Ethical Fashion Forum – now called Common Objective – and the

Centre for Sustainable Fashion at the London College of Fashion, run by the phenomenal Dilys Williams) followed shortly afterwards . . . and the rest, as they say, is history.

Within a few short months we were contacted by several individuals throughout the world, who had noticed our tiny Twitter presence, asking to become involved; and months later we welcomed Fashion Revolution Australia, Germany, Brazil and, increasingly, others into our growing family.

When I look back at the early days, I can honestly say that neither Carry nor I imagined that we would grow to become what is now (at the time of writing) the biggest fashion activism movement in the world – mostly because campaigning was not a part of our DNA, and we were very much making things up as we went along. I still believe that is one of the main reasons for our success: our spontaneity and the fact that we broke so many rules; our capacity to think as individuals rather than as a fully formed organization; the simplicity of the questions we were asking and the way we were asking them; our pro-fashion rather than anti-fashion stance; our irreverent (at the time) approach to branding and visual communication, which was celebratory and appealing rather than spelling out doom, gloom and destruction.

By the time we 'officially' came out into the world, on 24 April 2014 – exactly one year after the Rana Plaza catastrophe – we were already a force to be reckoned with. The collapse of Rana Plaza had shown everyone that our insatiable thirst for clothes (cheap or expensive), our impatience and the total disregard for human life resulting from our greed to consume have turned wearing clothes from a necessity into a lethal pastime: another stark reminder that our insatiable appetite for high-street fashion, for quantity over quality, for stuff we buy and often don't even bother to wear, is feeding on other people's misery.

The case for transparency is clear: if the brands sourcing from Rana Plaza had published their factory lists, if they themselves had known where they were producing in the first place and had made that information publicly available, the process for blame and the subsequent drive towards compensation would have been considerably faster; and active citizens would have been in a stronger position to demand better from the brands they trust.

The aftermath of the Rana Plaza collapse was felt throughout the world – the first real eye-opener for most consumers concerning exactly how much cheap clothing costs.

OTHER FASHION DISASTERS

The Rana Plaza disaster in Dhaka, Bangladesh, was the worst industrial disaster in the fashion industry by far: but it wasn't the first, and it won't be the last.

THE TRIANGLE SHIRTWAIST COMPANY
This factory fire in New York started on 25 March 1911, killing 145 workers. It is said that the fire started in a rag bag. The factory workers were made up mostly of teenage immigrant girls, speaking no English and working 12 hours a day for $15 a week. Due to the lack of a sprinkler system, blocked entrances and broken lifts, many workers burned to death or died jumping out of windows in desperation.

TAZREEN GARMENT-FACTORY FIRE
This fire broke out on 24 November 2012 in the Ashulia district on the outskirts of Dhaka, Bangladesh, killing 117 and injuring more than 200. While it is unclear how the fire started, the owner and several managers were charged with death, due to negligence. Rooms were cut off as piles of yarn and fabric-filled corridors ignited, and reports suggest that fire exits at the site were actually locked.

KARACHI GARMENT-FACTORY FIRE
The garment factory Ali Enterprises exploded into flames on 11 September 2012, killing 250 and seriously injuring 55. Many workers were trapped in the building, behind barred windows and locked exit doors. The building had no fire-fighting equipment, fire alarm or fire exits.

DELHI BAG-FACTORY FIRE
On 8 December 2019 a fire occurred at a school-bag-making factory in Delhi. Although it was the middle of the night, more than 100 garment workers, mostly migrants, were asleep on the factory floor; 43 victims died, with the youngest aged just 13.

CULTURE CHANGE

If it is true that fashion is an expression of who we are and of the culture we live in, then we need to respond to the profound moral questions that are defining this moment in time: pollution-driven climate heating, gender inequality, diversity and human rights.

Transparency isn't simply a system for sharing data; it is more than that – it is a start towards turning the industry inside out and upside down, a radical change in culture as well as practice. This whole industry thrives upon secrecy, and to open it wide for everyone to be a part of it, to encourage debate, criticism and positive activation, to put citizens in a position to demand better and to force brands to comply is no less than revolutionary.

It means diverting the focus from the product back to the people, and it will ultimately help consumers to make choices that are based on values, not just Instagram visibility. It is about protecting the real people who make up the industry, and safeguarding their working and living environment, which will ultimately have a beneficial effect on us all. It's about understanding how much, as consumers, we are prepared to compromise in order to own: are we really willing to keep ignoring deforestation, contamination and human exploitation?

In the absence of knowledge, it is easier to avoid asking further questions; in a transparent system, where visibility is provided as part of the parcel, concerned citizens can play an active part in ensuring that accurate information is being shared, compared and understood. In a radically transparent system, 'greenwashing' will become a thing of the past, as we will all have enough information to hand to make our own informed decisions.

Of course, one of the main concerns for critics is the fact that transparency and public accountability are self-disclosed; but self-disclosure within a culture of vigilance can be double-checked, and transparency provides the starting point to raise those questions that have gone unanswered, making brands responsible for providing that information and allowing consumers to accept, or reject, their claims.

Transparency and public disclosures measure the information that is provided, not the performance: a brand that isn't publicly disclosing is not necessarily one that isn't active in social and environmental practices; it simply means that they keep it to themselves. They might be talking about it extensively, but actively prevent their customers' engagement and their scrutiny. This is so typical of the fashion industry: exclusive, elusive, hidden. Transparency opens that door, so that you can put a foot in; so that it is your right to demand accountability, and see it progress over time.

Not all brands will be truthful, and not all citizens will care enough to find out, but it doesn't matter, because the people who are genuinely interested will be in a position to find out more and act upon it. And this certainly beats hands-down not having a clue! Most of all, by allowing consumers to compare brands on their social and environmental performances, it will encourage a healthier competitiveness than one that is based on profits alone. We want brands to compete to see who does the most good, not to see who sells the most goods.

Cultural changes don't happen overnight, and the system won't improve overnight, either, and this is precisely why we need to embrace this first step urgently, because by all accounts time is not on our side. Transparency will hasten this process if, while we firmly put it in place, we also look for other necessary improvements – from the micro to the macro – to happen at the same time. But first we need to foster the type of culture that will cradle these new attitudes: a culture that glorifies accountability, accuracy, abundance, quality and respect.

The fashion industry has an obligation to lead, and its potential to do better – and to inspire others to follow – is enormous. Time is running short and we need to act swiftly, but above all we need to act as a whole, because we all have a part to play.

Chapter 10

All Together Now

We have seen how the loss of our desire to make things last is having a negative effect on the planet. We know that we cannot keep buying cheap clothes just to throw them away; that we can no longer ignore the part we have to play.

We absolutely need to stop seeing our clothes as disposable. If only everyone knew how much time and energy goes into making them, we might slow down this unhealthy cycle of buying endlessly and, at times, needlessly. We have to find ways to break free from our addiction, reverse the throwaway culture and discover new ways to shop and care for our clothes.

Considering that the average lifespan of a modern-day piece of clothing is only 3.3 years, learning how to make and mend, or supporting those who do, is a brilliant investment – it will only take your time: your time to repair, recycle, repurpose, reinvent, reclaim, rescue and rewear. Far from being a part of the problem, we can all, enthusiastically and creatively, become a part of the solution.

You might now know more than you did before. And perhaps, as a result of reading this book, you will choose to take up some of my suggestions and put them into practice; hopefully, I have woken up the inner activist in at least some of you. Small actions undertaken by individuals, if multiplied by millions, can become a powerful tool for action. Sure, the biggest onus – the real responsibility for actual change – lies with higher powers, such as brands, corporations and governments, but people-power is essential.

The most important thing to do right now is to act collectively and speak up: to your family, friends and colleagues; speak truth to power – whatever that power might be – at your school, your workplace, your church, your gym, your local Sunday market. There is no better time than right now to push for change, and there is no better place to start than with your wardrobe. You can squeeze some simple daily practices into your life, month by month, and connect virtually, or IRL, with many others who are doing the same.

JANUARY
A New Year's resolution

'We only get change when we demand it. And if you don't see change you can believe in from a brand you support, take your money away and give it to someone who will take your priorities on board and help to change the industry for the better.'

Aja Barber, writer & style consultant

Funny old month, January: on the one hand we are supposed to set New Year's resolutions, which are almost always disciplined regimes, such as going to the gym, abstaining from alcohol, starting a vegan diet or detoxing from social-media overload, while on the other we are encouraged to buy just about anything we bump into in the January sales.

I resist both the constricting New Year's resolutions and the outright waste of the sales, on principle. Effectively, every January we're told to reinvent ourselves, and this really annoys me. Marketing messages tell us to lose weight, while sale season tells us to replenish our wardrobes, and a new calendar encourages us to put down all these concrete goals and start walking towards them, fast.

But what if, instead of telling ourselves that we need to start becoming a whole new person, we simply dedicate January to liking ourselves the way we are? Self-esteem is closely tied to our tendencies towards over-consumption, on so many different levels, so what if instead of 'New year, new me', our January mantra is one of contentment?

When it comes to the January sales, my trick to defy temptation is to turn the beast on its head and *use* the sales, as opposed to *being used* by them. That means buying something that I really need; buying sparingly as opposed to with abandon; and buying better, because the cheaper price affords me better quality, and quality equals longevity. I rigorously, exclusively buy only what I need: I don't go in for a pair of sneakers and come out with a flowery frock.

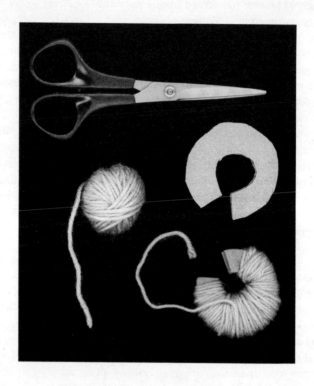

FEBRUARY
Carnival

'There's nothing interesting about looking perfect – you
lose the point. You want what you're wearing to say
something about you, about who you are.'
Emma Watson, actress & activist, *Teen Vogue*, 2009

In many countries, February is carnival month (this is huge in
Italy as in many other European countries, as well as in Brazil, of
course). Carnival, much like Halloween (more on that when we

get to October), has turned from a festival of creativity to one of mass consumption. Millions of cheap, plastic fancy-dress clothes are bought and discarded after being worn barely once. The result? Endless mini-*Frozen* costumes, thousands of plastic *Pirates of the Caribbean* swords and hats, countless Spider-Man outfits – the majority of which are made in utter misery, using miserably bad materials: you can find them in a landfill near you once the carnival is over.

Waste and unoriginality walk hand-in-hand in this case, with everybody looking so similar, as if no effort is made (maybe it isn't, unless walking to your local store and buying a ready-made costume can be considered an effort).

Arrange for a carnival party instead: get all your friends to join together for a messy 'making' afternoon, where costumes are created from scraps and unwanted clothes, from anything found, where anything goes. If you have kids, help them understand the value of playing with clothes as a form of self-expression; let their imaginations run riot and encourage them to create their own unique carnival characters.

BTW, the carnival party and that messy afternoon of making work just as well for a bunch of adults wanting to make an impression at the next fancy-dress party ;)

I have been lucky enough to win some awards for my fashion career in the past (the *Observer* Ethical Awards in 2010 and the *Elle* Style Awards 'Conscious Award' in 2017), but nothing beat the joy when my kids came home bearing a prize for some concoction of clothes that we used in order to make a costume. By far my most successful one was Slinky Malinki . . .

It was the easiest bit of dressing-up glory I have ever dreamed up, and all you need is black tights, a black jumper, a black feather boa (or a black scarf or tie) and a headband with ears (which you can also make yourself, by sticking two cardboard triangles to any old headband, tbh). Add black eyeliner-painted whiskers and a pink lipsticked little triangle on the nose tip, and it's done! If you don't have the feather boa/scarf, a really cute way of achieving something similar is by making lots of black pom-poms and tying them one after the other. Okay, it may be more poodle than cat, but who's going to notice?

MARCH
Women's month

> 'Fashion is part of our skin, and it's a political, social, economical, cultural voice for us.'
> Dominique Drakeford, writer & activist

Due to the success and global recognition of International Women's Day, which falls on 8 March, this month is widely regarded as 'women's month'.

Feminist and gender issues are inextricably linked with fashion, an industry that thrives on perfection over realism, idealization over diversity, with women's rights being violated at every step of the value chain, from factory floors to runway shows. So let's mark March as the month of acceptance, respect and repair, and use our clothes – and our sewing implements – as tools to send out a clear message: *We stand united.* It really doesn't have to turn into a big, splashy, sisterly moment; it can be as quiet and as simple as joining that quilting group, as you saw in Chapter 2, or giving someone you care about that piece in your wardrobe they've always been envious of, or finally passing on your vintage 1980s and '90s designer frocks that don't fit you any more to your daughter, who's been wanting them since she was six.

I owned a particular pair of oversized trousers – orange corduroy – bought in Rome in a vintage shop in the 1990s, which became a firm pregnancy favourite for myself, my best friend, her other best friend and then my daughter. We all left some mark or other: a white paint-splash happened, the button was changed, there's a tear that was stitched with red thread, seemingly in a hurry. To imagine that five babies were grown in those trousers is poetic to me: one pair of trousers, five pregnancies, five women for whom the sight of those trousers will forever be etched with their most intimate memories. I wonder who will wear them next.

Let's give our girlfriends our clothes, as well as a bunch of mimosas.

APRIL
Fashion Revolution Week

> 'If you don't like something, change it. If you cannot change it, change your attitude.'
> Maya Angelou, poet & civil-rights activist

The week that falls around 24 April is Fashion Revolution Week. Without a doubt, co-founding this movement has been my proudest professional achievement, and I still can't believe the growing numbers of people taking part in Fashion Revolution Week every year since we started it in 2014.

Fashion Revolution Week is as reflective as it is solutional and visionary. On 24 April each year we remember the victims of the tragic Rana Plaza collapse, and we reflect on what has changed in the industry since, and the work that remains to be done. Throughout the week there are thousands of events globally, and tens of thousands of individuals who act in unison to demand a fair fashion industry.

'Who made my clothes?' Ask this important question of the brands you have bought from this year. Whether you use your voice on social media or in an email or letter, Fashion Revolution Week is the time to stand up and demand greater industry transparency.

- ☞ **Get collective**: Fashion Revolution Week's success as a mover of the industry is due to its collective appeal. We know that change doesn't happen in a silo, and so we must bring people along with us whenever we engage in activism.
- ☞ **'What's in my clothes?'**: Understanding fabric composition can radically change the way we buy and care, so ask the brands that you trust for full disclosure on their restricted-substances policies, their chemical use and the traceability of all materials.
- ☞ **Tell your clothing love story**: As you may have gathered by now, I believe that clothes tell stories – like a personal journal, but potentially less secret. Share those stories with your friends and followers, and with a global community eager to make changes, as you are.

To find out more about Fashion Revolution Week, go to: fashionrevolution.org.

MAY
Summer swap party

> 'Fashion should never be tame. It should provoke, it
> should strive for spectacular innovation and expression:
> the fashion moment should hold magic. Fashion is risk,
> and should be.'
>
> Dr Mathilda Tham, design & future-studies professor

The month of May is perfect for a wardrobe reassessment and re-
arrangement, as you go from winter to summer (or from summer
to winter, for those in the Southern Hemisphere) and look at your
wardrobe's functionality. It's the perfect month for a swap party,
so that you and your friends and acquaintances can arrange ways
to refresh your wardrobes, without buying new.

How to organize a swap party at your home:

- ☞ Invite over your friends, family, neighbours, colleagues and
  co-workers.
- ☞ Set some ground rules to keep things organized: I suggest
  asking everyone to bring three pieces they no longer wear, but
  have once loved dearly. You can, of course, be less prescriptive
  with your emotional parameters and simply ask for three pieces
  that are in good nick.
- ☞ Once everyone arrives, hang the clothes and organize them
  by size and/or colour. (For the more advanced, why not hang
  according to fabric composition? Put all 100 per cent cotton, 100
  per cent poly, 100 per cent wool, etc., on one side, and all fabric
  blends on the other. That's a really good way to visualize all that
  you learned in Chapter 7, and how those garments will never be
  recycled, because being blends makes them unrecyclable. It's a
  great conversation starter!)
- ☞ Designate a trying-on area, with mirrors and privacy.
- ☞ Everyone should be allowed to swap three items, and once
  people have made their choices, those who brought unclaimed
  items should reclaim them, so as not to leave you with a surplus
  of unwanted clothes.

Clothing swaps are truly about reimagining how we engage with our clothes in a manner that doesn't revolve around consumption, but you can also use them as an opportunity to talk about clothing habits with your close friends. Share this book with them, and have everyone speak up about their challenges and solutions concerning their wardrobes.

If you enjoyed swapping clothes intimately among friends, you could try your hand at doing it on a larger scale: at your workplace, your kids' school, your local church or library.

This is similar to a home swap, but you'll need some friends or volunteers to help manage the larger space and the bigger influx of clothing. To attract more people for the community swap, it's a great idea to advertise on social media, or to design and print some posters. You can make your swap even more re-purposeful by having mending stations for damaged or imperfect goods, or by inviting local tailors and sewers to offer their services.

JUNE
Wedding season

'Elegance is refusal.'
Coco Chanel, fashion designer

June typically kicks off the summer wedding season in the Northern Hemisphere, which is a major trigger for single-use clothing consumption. In 2019 Oxfam commissioned a study discovering that the British population will purchase more than 50 million single-use outfits for summertime in a given year. Of these, 9.9 million outfits are attributed to wedding-season frocks: garments and outfits that will only be worn once. As the pressure to look good, and to look different every time, takes its toll on your wallet and on the environment, renting or sharing with your friends becomes a real solution.

☞ **Buy second-hand**: Find a unique piece that will have the congregation showering compliments on you like confetti, and avoid the embarrassing moment when you turn up in the same dress as someone else. After all, weddings are about eternal love and, as such, the idea of wearing a dress that will never be worn again looks like the most hypocritical kind of fashion statement.

☞ **Rent your gown**: These days rental services have multiplied like mushrooms – from huge portals such as Y Closet in China and Rent the Runway in the USA, to smaller start-ups such as My Wardrobe in the UK. It will be easy to find them online.

☞ **Share with others**: Chances are that if you have a line-up of summer weddings to attend, so do your friends and families. Why not share a summer wardrobe between you? As teenagers, sisters, cousins and friends have a tendency to share their clothing and borrow from one another's wardrobes, I think it is a grave mistake that we outgrow this delightful habit. At any age – come wedding season or any other season – we should open up our wardrobes to one another and swap outfits. *What's mine is yours, friends.*

That same Oxfam study highlighted summer festivals as the generator of another 7.4 million single-use outfits. As music festivals have risen to become showcases for style and fashion fads, the temptation to buy a boho dress or a cowboy hat – things that perhaps aren't your style but feel like an appropriate costume – is palpable. But music festivals, which often hold a certain kind of New Age energy, are generally places of acceptance, so it seems fitting that we should dress for them in the clothes we love most – clothes that best represent us, clothes we already own.

JULY
Bikini body

'Buy less, choose well and make it last.'
Vivienne Westwood, fashion designer

Beware of your bikini – it might be leaving a more indelible mark than just your tan line. Bikinis, and swimsuits, are made of synthetic fibres such as nylon and polyester, highly contaminating materials that have disastrously negative effects on all living species on Planet Earth, but on marine life in particular. If we keep buying cheap bikinis each time we go on holiday and chucking them after one week's usage, we are contributing to the pollution of those same lovely waters that we are swimming in.

I am not suggesting we should all be bathing in organic cotton, but there are way better alternatives out there than your average cheap bikini: you can look for recycled polyester and recycled nylon as an option (see also Chapter 5, and look out for econyl, which is made from recycled nylon); or you can buy one or two swimsuits and care for them properly, so that you don't have to buy new ones, come the next holiday.

☞ Care well: Caring for your swimwear is no more laborious than rinsing your hair, but just as important for its maintenance. All it takes is a quick wash after each daily use in a bowl of warm (fresh) water, regardless of whether you swam in the sea or in a swimming pool. I add a minuscule drop of hand-washing detergent (literally the size of a pinhead), but shampoo will do instead. And I keep wearing my bikinis year in, year out.

☞ Buy well: In all honesty, investing in a well-cut, well-made swimsuit (and caring for it) is absolutely worth it, and infinitely more flattering than sporting the latest trends. I have had four children, and I know all too well the saggy bits that I prefer to be reined in, the neckline that needs to stay put, the gentle squeeze that works with my shape and gives me confidence, rather than making me feel like a sausage. All my swimwear was good-quality in the first place (I even still have a few costumes that were my mother's!) and they still do what they are supposed to do: hold me, in more ways than one.

I'm not going to bother you with 'activities' and stuff to do – it's July, you can have a break! Mending is often uncomfortable during the hot summer months (who wants an extra layer of clothing sitting on your lap?), but maybe you can use your downtime not only to enjoy the latest bestseller, but also to dig deeper into some of the stuff you read about here, and keep honing your clothes-keeper's knowledge.

AUGUST
Getting ready to go back to school

> 'The century and scenes and actors may
> change, but the struggle remains the same:
> for dignity, for a living wage, for a safe
> workplace, for bread, and for roses, too.'
> Kim Kelly, *Teen Vogue*

August in the Northern Hemisphere is time for the back-to-school shopping tour de force that most parents face every year; as our stuff becomes cheaper – in price and quality – it's harder to make it last from year to year, or from child to child. In the UK, school uniforms are largely made from cheap synthetic fibres, and the drive to make them less expensive allows for all sorts of unethical practices in the supply chain.

In 2014 the supermarket giant ASDA announced that it was selling a school uniform for less than £10 – including the shoes. Preparing for the scholastic year ahead can be a massive burden. No wonder we need to buy cheap. Although there are certifications to seek out in school uniforms, and indeed all clothes – like GOTS certified organic cotton, or recycled yarns – the best thing we can do is swap and share, to keep these clothes in circulation.

Most schools run second-hand uniform sales, but, if yours doesn't, hold one yourself! Reach out to the parents across the school years and urge them to donate the uniform (or school-appropriate clothes, if there is no uniform) their kids have grown out of. Arrange the items by age/size and type, price them cheaply and donate the profits back to the school.

Otherwise, think twice before you buy new, and see if there isn't some old life left in last year's school attire, which could be spruced back to life with some basic alterations or upcycling tricks. Maybe your child has experienced a growth spurt, and taking down a hemline is enough to make those trousers, or skirt, last until Christmas? Could you not cut down a pair of sweatpants that are a little bit too short and snug and turn them into shorts? A very basic hem will stop any fringing and make them look as neat as new. You can make long-sleeved shirts that are damaged at the elbows or wrists into short-sleeved shirts, and remove the sleeves of a sweatshirt completely to make it into a sleeveless one.

SEPTEMBER
#SecondHandSeptember

'Shopping second-hand and wearing second-hand clothes is a magical bond between you and what has gone before you. You may not always know the stories held between the threads and love lines of a piece but you know it has a story before you and that the next chapter is yours, and that's pretty cool.'

Emma Slade Edmondson, strategic creative consultant

Oxfam's global initiative asks us to embrace second-hand clothing during the month of September: although many of us may already love to thrift, and do this all year round, the campaign is the perfect opportunity to bring your friends into the fold. Find a friend whose style you like, and go second-hand clothes shopping together. Make a rule that you both have to try on three things selected by the other, and go for it! The aim isn't necessarily to buy, but to try new styles and rediscover all the beautiful clothes that already exist.

Supporting campaigns such as Oxfam's 'Second Hand September' is important because it adds your voice – your small, inconspicuous, random, maybe even slightly embarrassed voice – to thousands of others, making it a collective roar. Even if you're not the type of person who embraces campaigns, wearing an item of clothing bought at a charity shop and maybe talking a little bit about why you have chosen to wear it – on social media or to your friends – is hardly the same as declaring a lifetime allegiance to Extinction Rebellion.

OCTOBER
Halloween

'There is no beauty in the finest cloth if it
makes hunger and unhappiness.'
Mahatma Gandhi, politician & social activist

As a mother to four kids (and grandmother to two) I do have
a speciality: the dressing-up box. Anything I no longer want
(and some things I very much still want, but have to concede are
better for dressing up than for real life) goes in it. I have been
blessed with extremely creative children, each and every one of
them perfectly capable of rustling up any costume, any character (real or imagined), using anything from discarded clothes to
cardboard boxes; but I have seen some of their friends, not quite
so accustomed to clothing mayhem, being less confident with
trash-styling. So I often curate piles of clothing especially for a
Halloween dressing-up party: a pile of black (including broken
tights, scarves, socks, old T-shirts and ties) is great for a classic
witch, and most of my husband's torn shirts (the ones I haven't
already turned into nighties) and jackets go into the *Inspector
Gadget* pile; sparkly stuff for fairies, and beiges, greens, reds,
pinks, lilacs and pale blues for princesses.

This next Halloween alone more than 2,000 tonnes of plastic will be consumed and discarded, for the sake of one night of
entertainment in the UK alone. Please, please let's curb this madness at least. Why not get together after the summer and work
with local primary schools to create curated Halloween dressing-
up boxes from your discarded clothes?

PARTNERING UP WITH YOUR LOCAL SCHOOL TO CREATE HALLOWEEN DRESSING-UP BOXES

This is ideal if you have children at nursery/kindergarten or primary school who partake in 'mufti day' – a day when the kids get to wear whatever they want to school, provided they bring in a small donation to a chosen charity. But it can also be a hilarious initiative that you can implement for university students and even at your workplace.

- ☞ Every parent/participant creates one or two fancy-dress costume boxes, using stuff they already have at home. Boxes are clearly labelled with the character and age range that the contents are suitable for: for example, 'sparkly witch, ages 4–6' or 'psycho clown just escaped from jail, age 18+'.
- ☞ The children/participants bring their boxes into school/uni/work and spend the morning swapping boxes and dressing up.
- ☞ At the end of the day, unwanted costume boxes get returned to whoever donated them.

NOVEMBER
Black Friday

'It's only waste because we waste the
opportunity to turn it into something else.'
will-i-am, rapper & songwriter,
'Let's make plastic a verb', *The Guardian*, 3 October 2013

Don't believe the hype. Black Friday, Singles Day, Cyber Monday . . . driving attention to a system that glorifies excess during a time of catastrophic climate breakdown is utterly irresponsible, especially considering how far we have come in exposing waste, surplus and super-cheap discounts as being a massive part of the problem. Plus, it's a lie. We are not hunting for a bargain, we're being overloaded with prey.

A recent article published in *The Guardian* newspaper showed that just one in 20 Black Friday deals is genuine, according to damning research by *Which?* It concluded that the annual shopping event was 'all hype'. 'We have repeatedly shown that "deals" touted by retailers on Black Friday are not as good as they seem. Time-limited sales can be a good opportunity to bag a bargain, but don't fall for the pressure tactics around Black Friday,' said Natalie Hitchins, *Which?*'s head of home products and services.

We should look towards alternatives, and keep inventing new ways to antagonize these semi-hysterical cheap shopping bonanzas. I propose 'Fix Friday' rather than Black Friday – who's with me? Gather your friends in protest and organize a mending circle instead.

I have recently organized two 'Stitch and Bitch' events: one in person, where participants came along with their needlework and sat together chatting and sewing; and one on Zoom, where all participants joined virtually from their homes, and we proceeded as normal – stitching and bitching, only virtually! It worked just as well.

You could also use your social media and tag the brands whose clothes you are mending; demand better-quality products; demand consumer extended guarantees and repair services; make a noise against mindless consumerism.

The Saturday after Black Friday has been colloquially named 'Small Business Saturday' in an effort to encourage consumers to support their local businesses as an alternative to the big-box sales of the cyber weekend. Supporting local is a beautiful action in any manner, but it doesn't need to be solely about buying new things from local makers or boutiques. Small Business Saturday can also be about supporting local clothing services. Head to your local cobbler and get a pair of shoes re-soled, or visit your local tailor for a much-needed alteration.

DECEMBER
Christmas shedding vs Christmas shopping

> 'An ugly Christmas sweater, worn for a giggle
> and then chucked aside, may not make or break
> the climate crisis, but it's a microcosm of a
> larger problem.'
> Jasmin Malik Chua, *Teen Vogue*

My family is known for our excessive gift-giving Christmas extravaganzas, and many friends who have been invited to our legendary Christmas Eves have commented that they have never seen such a display of abundance. I am not joking – the entire sitting room can be covered in gifts.

Our secret is Christmas shedding, as opposed to Christmas shopping: we give each other our own things, keeping loved objects in circulation for years and years. This tradition was started by my mother and her sister, who began by adding to their 'bought' gifts some of their own pre-owned trinkets (it could be anything: an old picture frame, a piece of jewellery, items of vintage clothing, cups and saucers, books . . .), until we all realized that those were always the favourite presents. And so they somewhat took over from the bought stuff, to take centre-stage during gift-giving moments.

And no wonder! I mean, how much can you say about a bottle of perfume bought in a department store? What's the story behind it? On the other hand, imagine my 80-year-old mother gifting her 1960s studded belt to her teenage grandson – you can talk about that for hours and remember it for ever. The secret to successful shedding is to gift something you still like, something you are attached to, something you will be happy to see worn or used by someone you love, even though you may still have feelings for it. That's the poignancy of it all, and why it feels so special.

Of course, Christmas is not only about 25 December, but the whole social build-up that accompanies it, with office parties, cocktail drinks and dinners. I guess it's the same dilemma as the wedding season – how often you can bear to be seen wearing the same outfit. My answer is: *As often as you like!*

It is virtuous to keep rewearing things, and it's smart: if you have a dress that is already your body's best friend (and there aren't many of those around in your lifetime), why not keep wearing it? Why not keep showing yourself in your best light? Because a dress that suits your shape, and your principles, will make you glow. I suggest something simple, something so flattering it looks like you were born to wear it, which you can style and restyle again and again by switching accessories, like a blank canvas that accommodates your every whim.

And if you haven't met such a dress yet (keep looking for it) . . . rent or borrow.

We are caught in a vicious cycle of excess, of disrespecting nature, as opposed to a virtuous cycle of living in symbiosis with it. We are pushing the natural boundaries of our planet, and we have gone too far. We have lost the past 20 years to climate-breakdown deniers, and to our collective inability and lack of determination to commit to changes that we now know to be necessary. We turned a blind eye – it's wake-up time.

Iconic fashion journalist Sarah Mower wrote, 'Revolutions happen slowly and then all at once, in a rush, and then they become inevitable', and this is exactly what we are seeing now: this inevitability and urgency to act, which is so frightening, so daunting.

Undoubtedly it would have been much better if we had acted in time, if we had prevented the current state of affairs, but we didn't; and in many respects we still aren't – not enough anyway. Respecting nature and all its living creatures (and that means each other, too) is the only way. It's time to act: *Best foot forward*, as they say.

And what does that foot look like? It's wearing a shoe that has been regularly re-soled, made with non-chromium or vegan leather of the highest quality. Inside that shoe is a sock – an organic cotton sock that is about to break, and which will be used to experiment with darning, since you have decided that you want to learn how. Grazing the shoe is a hemline which belongs to a pair of trousers that are well made and much loved, perhaps bought second-hand or hand-made by a local tailor. Tucked into the trousers is your best friend's designer silk shirt. As you walk out of the house you put on your beautiful recycled polyester overcoat, a treasured investment that you saved up for last year, which you spot-cleaned and refreshed with a steam this morning.

Keep the clothes you have with pride, minimize new acquisitions and do it with the kind of infectious enthusiasm that radiates joy and personal fulfilment – one that others close to you will follow.

Because the only things we need more of right now are trees and whales and birds and bees – not clothes.

Further
Reading

BOOKS

Baskets
Tabara N'Diaye (2019)

Clothing Poverty
Andrew Brooks (2015)

The Conscious Closet
Elizabeth L. Cline (2019)

Cradle to Cradle
Michael Braungart & William McDonough (2002)

The Craft of Use
Kate Fletcher (2016)

Deluxe
Dana Thomas (2007)

Dress with Sense
Christina Dean (2017)

Earth Logic
Kate Fletcher & Mathilda Tham (2019)

Emotionally Durable Design
Jonathan Chapman (2005)

Fibershed
Rebecca Burgess (2019)

Fixing Fashion
Michael Lavergne (2015)

The Golden Thread
Kassia St Clair (2018)

Green Is the New Black
Tamsin Blanchard (2007)

How to Be a Craftivist
Sarah Corbett (2017)

How to Start Sewing
Assembil Books (2016)

I Can Make Shoes
Amanda Overs (2019)

Mending Matters
Katrina Rodabaugh (2018)

No Logo
Naomi Klein (1999)

No Patterns Needed
Rosie Martin (2016)

Overdressed
Elizabeth L. Cline (2012)

Refashioned
Sass Brown (2013)

Rise & Resist
Clare Press (2018)

The Routledge Handbook
of Sustainability & Fashion
*Kate Fletcher &
Mathilda Tham (2014)*

Sewing Basics For Every Body
Wendy Ward (2020)

Slave to Fashion
Safia Minney (2017)

Slow Fashion
Safia Minney (2016)

The Slow Grind
Georgina Johnson (2020)

Stitched Up
Tansy E. Hoskins (2014)

The Story of Stuff
Annie Leonard (2010)

Stuffocation
James Wallman (2013)

The Subversive Stitch
Rozsika Parker (2010)

This Changes Everything
Naomi Klein (2014)

Threads of Life
Clare Hunter (2019)

Wardrobe Crisis
Clare Press (2016)

Weave This
*Francesca Kletz &
Brooke Dennis (2018)*

Why Materials Matter
Seetal Solanki (2018)

FILMS & DOCUMENTARIES

Before the Flood
Fisher Stevens (2016)

Made in Bangladesh
Rubaiyat Hossain (2019)

The Price of Free
Derek Doneen (2018)

RiverBlue
Roger Williams &
David McIlvride (2017)

The True Cost
Andrew Morgan (2015)

ZINES, PUBLICATIONS & ONLINE RESOURCES

Action Required
Fashion Revolution
fashionrevolution.org

Clean Clothes Campaign
cleanclothes.org

Dead White Man's Clothes
Liz Ricketts & Branson Skinner
deadwhitemansclothes.org

Fashion Craft Revolution
Fashion Revolution
fashionrevolution.org

Fashion Environment Change
Fashion Revolution
fashionrevolution.org

Fashion Open Studio
Fashion Revolution
fashionopenstudio.com

Fashion and Race Database
Kimberly Jenkins
fashionandrace.com

Good on You
goodonyou.eco

The Higg Index
Sustainable Apparel Coalition
apparelcoalition.org/the-higg-index/

Loved Clothes Last
Fashion Revolution
fashionrevolution.org

Melanin and Sustainable Style
Dominique Drakeford
melaninass.com

Money Fashion Power
Fashion Revolution
fashionrevolution.org

Save Your Wardrobe
www.saveyourwardrobe.com

Acknowledgements

I could not have written this book without the practical help and emotional support of my daughter, Elisalex de Castro Peake, and of Bronwyn Seier. They were with me every step of the way throughout this challenging but wonderful process, researching, correcting and contributing – I am beyond grateful.

I also want to thank my agent, Kate Evans at Peters Fraser + Dunlop, for 'discovering' me on Instagram and giving me this incredible opportunity (secretly hoped for, but never anticipated), and for her help and support throughout; and my editor, Emily Robertson, for trusting me and encouraging me.

My biggest thank you goes to my husband Filippo, for absolutely everything really; and to my family, especially for bearing with me while I was writing, swinging wildly between every emotion possible.

Thank you to the women with whom I have shared clothes, and whose clothes reside in my wardrobe: my grandmothers Nonna Stanilla and Nonna Mussi, my mother, my aunt Zia Giovanna, my cousins Francesca, Aurora, Maria Novella e Bianca. Thank you to my friend Nena, extreme clothes-sharing with me since 1980. And also to Sarah and Ondine – I will miss you for ever.

A massive thank you to Anna Orsini, mentor and friend, for opening up so many professional doors for me, generously and protectively – Estethica at London Fashion Week was a pivotal moment for sustainable fashion, and it couldn't have happened without you and the British Fashion Council; and to Donatella Barrigelli, remembering our shared From Somewhere adventures, and all the pioneering clothes we made together; thank you to Sasha Schwerdt, for starting the label with me; and to Silvia Bocchese Stein and M.I.L.E.S., for opening up a whole new waste stream and kick-starting my call.

Thank you to all who worked at From Somewhere, and to the skilled workers who made our clothes.

Thank you to everyone at Fashion Revolution, in particular Carry Somers, for sharing her idea with me to make it our vision; but also to Sarah Ditty, Heather Knight, Jocelyn Whipple, Roxanne Houshmand, Lucy Shea, Martine Parry and Ian Cook, for building its foundations; and thank you to Tamsin Blanchard, for joining us after many years of unparalleled support on all fronts.

Thank you also to all the Fashion Revolution Global Teams around the world.

Thank you to Renata Molcho, Katharine Hamnett, Sam Robinson, Suzy Menkes, Sara Maino, Dilys Willams, Christina Dean, Baronass Lola Young, Willi Walters, Maria Nishio, Leslie Johnston, Marina Spadafora, Lucy Siegle, Sarah Mower and Céline Semaan.

Thank you to my brothers, Vittorio and Lorenzo, and to my sister-in-law Ottavia, for my wonderful nieces, Giulia, Margherita and Clementina.

Index